D0437252

SOUR GRIPES

SOUR GRIPES

Crazy claims and ridiculous rulings
guaranteed to blow your fuses

SIMON CARR

PORTRAIT

Visit the Portrait website!

PORTRAIT

Portrait publishes a wide range of non-fiction, including biography, history, science, music, popular culture and sport.

Visit our website to:
- read descriptions of our popular titles
- buy our books over the internet
- take advantage of our special offers
- enter our monthly competition
- learn more about your favourite Portrait authors

VISIT OUR WEBSITE AT: www.portraitbooks.com

First published in Great Britain in 2006 by
Portrait, an imprint of
Piatkus Books Ltd
5 Windmill Street, London W1T 2JA
email: info@piatkus.co.uk

The moral right of the author has been asserted
A catalogue record for this book is available from the British Library

ISBN 0 7499 5119 2

Text design by Andy Summers, Planet Creative
Illustrations by Simon Pearsall

This book has been printed on paper manufactured
with respect for the environment using wood from
managed sustainable resources

Typeset by Phoenix Photosetting, Chatham, Kent
www.phoenixphotosetting.co.uk
Printed and bound in Great Britain by
Mackays of Chatham, Chatham, Kent

Lawyers are the worst people in the world at figuring out right from wrong. They only like to talk about what the law says, not what common sense says. If you want to know what's right and what's wrong, ask a child.

Celia Farber, New York Press

Contents

Contents

Introduction

On the towpath of the Oxford Canal, just where the narrow boats moor near the centre of town, I came across a large, irritable, white swan. It was so out of place – being wild, and unregulated – that I couldn't believe it was legal. It was hissing and stretching its neck and making pecking movements at cyclists. That's surely not acceptable in a built-up area, is it? Shouldn't I call some government agency to report it? Have its licence withdrawn?

That's what we've come to in Britain. A wild swan is so out of place on a canal towpath that even someone like me considers reporting it to the authorities for the sake of public order.

When you look around Britain, this Brave New World is everywhere you turn. We now live in a country where children can't have a pancake race without public liability insurance. Almost every sort of public gathering has to be supervised, overseen, marshalled. It all has to be permitted, in writing, by the police, the council the – I don't know – the Health and Safety

Executive. The numbers have to be limited by insurance. And why? Because any accident is liable to produce a court case to see if compensation is due to the person who was hurt, or to their distressed family and possibly to the public-service workers who attended the accident.

The world changes, and not always for the worse. People now have access to the legal system in a way we didn't when I was young. That's got to have a good side to it. The authorities are also a lot more careful about their relations with members of the public. They can get sued if they're not. We can hit back at our masters, our bosses, our administrative overlords. That's all to do with this compensation culture, so-called, that has sprung up in the last generation.

So, I'm not against it all, not by any means. Like you, I'm in favour of justice. But, if the law gets out of whack with what most people feel is fair, then there's a problem.

This book is a collection of stories, reports, summaries, Parliamentary exchanges and extracts from depositions that show a compensation system out of whack with what most reasonable people think is fair.

Some of the items make me laugh out loud, and it's easier to make a cat laugh, frankly, after all these years. I hope you find enough in here to make you laugh as well. Or howl. Or howl at the moon. There's something for everyone.

Where there's blame there's a claim

Some of these examples are bizarre. But the bizarre isn't interesting unless it illuminates some general truth. For the most bizarre general truths, you have to go to America. Try this.

The World Trade Center was first bombed back in 1993. Islamic terrorists parked a vanload of explosives in the underground car park and let it off, killing six and wounding nearly 1,000. Who was to blame? A New York jury found that the people who were mainly and overwhelmingly to blame (68 per cent to blame, to be precise) were the American owners of the building. The terrorists who had bought, planted and detonated the explosives? They were only 28 per cent responsible.

Because the owners (the New York Port Authority) were found more than half responsible, they became liable for all the damages ($1.8 billion was sought).

It helps to know that it wasn't much use to find the bombers were mainly responsible for the bombing. They weren't available to pay, and, even if they were, they almost certainly don't have $1.8 billion in the bank.

It'll never get that bad in Britain, not unless we abolish the loser-pays rule in civil cases, and not until we allow juries to allocate damages.

No, we don't have a US-style compensation culture. We have a UK-style compensation culture, which is a very different thing. For instance, if my 17-year-old son found a rat in a hamburger, he would be delighted. It would make his month. The opportunity to make a fuss would be unique. He'd have a story for the rest of his life with the world's best punchline: 'And inside the bun, there was the head of a rat! And its eyes were still open!' Mind you, Mrs Mohamad of Ontario (see Chapter 10) must have been delighted as well: 'A rat in a hamburger! That'll be $20 million, please!'

My personal experience of compensation is limited but dramatic.

Thirty years before the time of writing this – 35 years, now I think about it – I was working in a moulding factory in Harpenden. We were making plastic bits. I never found out why, or what they were. You didn't ask in those days. The machine closed every 40 seconds and squirted hot plastic in through its chambers. Fifty tons of pressure kept the mould closed and then it clanged open with a bump, spilling out the bits. But the mechanism was always sticking, and a nut always needed to be tightened. Turning the machine off was an awful fag and there were 40 seconds in the cycle, so I used to tighten the bolt while the thing was running.

You can probably tell what's coming up. Sensitive readers should look away now. One day, I was standing on the far side of the guard gate while reaching into the machine. My body pushed the gate back, broke the electronic contact and the machine opened. I couldn't see what was happening but I noticed I couldn't pull my hand out of the works. I tugged and couldn't get out; I thought my sleeve had got caught. That could be dangerous! I managed to get round and look in, and there was my crucified hand, pierced by a fat, metal bolt. The fingers twitched a bit, I noticed, like a spider's legs, with its body crushed by some precise sort of nail head.

I scrabbled at the buttons, making a gargling sound; for some reason, the panic cleared and I saw the right button very clearly, pressed it, retrieved my hand and lifted it up. I could see daylight through the palm. The fingers are still twisted a bit, and when it gets cold I have no feeling on the inside edges of my third and fourth fingers.

The company paid six weeks' wages (no overtime). The physiotherapist hurt me more than the machine had (times were very different). We thought about suing, and even got in touch with a solicitor. But I couldn't be bothered with the forms. Even I had to admit it had been a dangerous thing to do. Had the owners warned me not to put my hand into the machine while it was still running? It was one of those things people didn't feel it was necessary to say in those days. Or maybe they did tell me, and I ignored them. Even after the accident, I'd probably have done it again, but with more care. That's what things were like, for better or worse, in the days before a compensation culture.

As for my compensation, there wasn't much of that then. There isn't much of it now, in fact, not for mere accidents. I'd be lucky to get £5,000 if it happened tomorrow (about what I got then, in fact, adjusted for inflation). I never got past the solicitor stage for a civil claim (as I say, the forms were too boring).

No, for the compensation you read about in newspapers you have to know what to say, how to reconstruct the situation and what to feel. The culture has developed quite a strict code, which you have to conform to if you want the big bucks. It has to 'ruin your life'. You would need to 'consider suicide'. You must suffer long-term psychological damage from the incident, and, if you haven't suffered that damage immediately, you'd better make sure you suffer it subsequently. Of course, you can damage yourself very thoroughly, if it's worth your while.

Sting in the tail

A lot of eminent people deny there is a compensation culture at all in this country. Some of them are fierce. A Labour MP (and personal-injury lawyer) talked out a perfectly reasonable cross-party Bill in Parliament, say-ing it was 'an unlimited charter to injure, kill and maim young children'. All sorts of special interests (including the government's absurdly named Better Regulation Taskforce) denounce the 'myth' of a com-pensation culture. It's all been got up by the media, they say.

6

Even the Lord Chancellor has said that claims fell by 10 per cent in 2005 and therefore we didn't have a compensation culture in this country.

In the old-fashioned phrase, they should get out more.

A friend of mine is a disability officer in an educational institution. She has to arrange visits from a dozen old-age pensioners at a time and has to send out forms that have to be filled in before they arrive (they never are). One old lady stood up in her inaugural group and announced that she was allergic to wasps and if she was stung she would die unless she was injected with the serum (which she produced in one hand) via a hypodermic (in her other hand).

My friend was obliged to point out that if she were indeed stung by a wasp no one would be allowed to inject her. If the old lady died, anyone physically involved could be sued for compensation by any surviving relatives. It was legally possible for others to help the old lady 'into the recovery position'. They could, if brave, help her to inject herself (assuming she hadn't succumbed to anaphylactic shock). But to take control of the hypodermic without a current, recognised qualification would render the helper liable for civil suit. No, the proper procedure is to put her in 'the recovery position', phone for qualified help, and watch her die.

The deep legal background of my friend's ruling is unimportant. It is the official advice; it is the advice that is given out; people act on it. Maybe it is absolutely right in law, or maybe the Health and Safety ruling she's been given is overcautious. But who wants to take a case to the House of Lords to find out?

Try this other one. A friend of mine was on a plane travelling to Cuba. One of the passengers had quite a serious turn. 'Is there a qualified medical professional on the plane?' the call went out. Three people came forward: a paramedic, a nurse, an orthopaedic surgeon. They were asked to produce their qualifications.

Of course they didn't have them to hand; they were in a plane cabin. They were told to resume their seats. They couldn't even offer advice. The cabin crew practically put their hands over their ears and went 'La-la-la-la-la!' in case they heard anything that a court could construe as having influenced them. They radioed ahead and took advice over the phone from a duty doctor.

There's no question in my mind that a compensation culture exists in this country. It's not as bad as in other countries, and it may have been checked in the last couple of years (or it may not, we don't know). But it unquestionably exists. Not only does it exist, it's grown exponentially from almost nothing in the last 25 years or so to an industry many times larger than BP. Its turnover is – I'm going to pluck a figure out of the air, as everybody else does – about £50 billion a year in claims, costs, lost earnings and benefits.

That figure dwarfs previous estimates from the Institute of Actuaries but – having looked into it – I see that the effects of a compensation culture are much more widespread than people have thought, and they reach into unexpected areas of modern life.

You'll see the effects in those odd items you read about in the newspapers (some of which are true). You see it in the million skivers (or malingerers or victims) on incapacity benefit who say they want to work, but don't. You see it in the hot-shot City 'burn-outs' who take advantage of their income-replacement insurance to take to the golf course. You see it in the fact that GPs are now 13 times more likely to face negligence claims than they were ten years ago. You see it in the fact that claims now cost the NHS £500 million a year (whereas 30 years ago it was £7 million in today's money, and less than ten years ago it was only £50 million).

The other important point is that nobody has any real idea of how big this culture is, or what it actually costs. We can only sense the extent of it by considering the following questions (most of which are unanswerable).

- How many policemen and firefighters have taken early retirement with a 'bad back'?

- How many teachers' hours have been taken up by schools defending claims from parents whose children bumped their heads in the playground?

- Why did Surrey police spent £9,000 in the course of a year to send drunks home in a taxi?

- Why won't nursery schools administer medicine to their little pupils?

- Why can't teachers touch children?

- How many NHS hours are taken up dealing with the 95 per cent of claims that never get to arbitration?

- Why are hundreds of thousands of tombstones lying flat in cemeteries all over Britain?

- Why do many local authorities pay more to people who've slipped and tripped than on maintaining the pavements that cause slips and trips?

- Why did that teacher seek a million pounds from Bristol Council because her chair made an embarrassing noise whenever she sat down?

- Why did the police wait an hour and seven minutes before entering a Henley flat and let two women bleed to death while witnesses pleaded for the women's lives?

- Why has the number of people claiming incapacity benefit trebled in a generation when public health is inexorably improving?

The sheer existential fact of a compensation culture is illustrated most poignantly by one story.

Forty years ago, a slag heap above a Welsh mining village became unstable. Part of it broke away to slide into Aberfan. It was an avalanche of mud, spoil and industrial waste thundering down into the mining village. On the outskirts of the village, the children of the primary school had just finished singing 'All Things Bright and Beautiful' and had returned to their desks. Four years later, a 12-year-old girl described what she then experienced:

'It was a tremendous rumbling sound and all the school went dead. You could hear a pin drop. Everyone just froze in their seats. I just managed to get up and I reached the end of my desk when the sound got louder and nearer, until I could see the black out of the window. I can't remember any more but I woke up to find that a horrible nightmare had just begun in front of my eyes.'

The slurry swamped the school, drowning and crushing half the children and five of their teachers. Twenty houses in the village were destroyed. In all, 116 children and 28 adults were killed. The last survivor was pulled out of the rubble in under two hours; it took a week to retrieve all the bodies. It's hard to read the stories that come out of that episode without your feelings welling up in your eyes.

Compensation paid for each dead child was set at £500. It was about the price of a cattle beast. The National Coal Board called it 'a generous offer'. The Board eventually paid £160,000 to the villagers, but insisted on a repayment of £150,000 from the disaster

11

charitable trust (they wanted financial help to move the slag heaps). Even by the standards of those *Life on Mars* days, they behaved abominably. Every official involved retired with full honours.

Nonetheless, in spite of the incompetence, malevolence and corporate buck passing, the villagers collectively voted not to sue the Board. That would be to 'bow to vengeance'.

And then the culture changed. A generation later, in 1990, a woman issued a writ against the Board for psychological damage suffered by witnessing the event. She got more than anyone who'd been hurt at the time.

And jolly good thing too, some might say. You may be right. Let's leave that aside for a moment. The fact is that a compensation culture clearly didn't exist at the time of the disaster, but clearly did exist by the time the woman sued 25 years later.

So, there we are. I hope that's settled the question. In that spirit, let's proceed with the first, enjoyable, part of this book with a lot of stories that make our blood boil, just to rub in the actual fact that this compensation culture exists. Then for the sake of balance (because this book isn't anti-compensation) we'll look at a number of cases that really deserve compensation (there are some stinkers out there).

There is a feeling that the high-water mark of claims has now stabilised, as a result of a couple of Law Lords' decisions. That's an interesting element of the mix — cultures can, and do, change quite rapidly.

Is that worth £9.99? Some may think it is and some may think it isn't. If you feel short-changed, get your solicitor to write to mine and we can get to know each other better.

Quick Run-Around

Some of these examples will be more familiar than others. Some will be more true than others. Court cases are always more complex than the reports of court cases. Watching *LA Law*, or even *Crown Court*, one would find it striking how one's sympathies would swing from one witness to another. Matters of fact were important, but also – shame on us – whether the people were likable.

As a nine-year-old child, Carl Murphy broke into a warehousing unit near Liverpool, climbed up onto its roof, fell 40 feet to a concrete floor and fractured his skull. He was partially blinded in one eye and had 17 metal plates holding his skull together.

He and his grandmother (who looked after him while his parents were in prison for crack dealing) say the accident caused him behavioural problems. It was unclear whether these problems included his shaving his head, making the scars more prominent, and intimidating local residents.

On turning 18 in 2005, he sued the owner of the warehouse for compensation. Damages were owing to him, he claimed, because, if the site had a better security fence to keep him out, he wouldn't have been injured. The grandmother was quoted as saying, 'He never finished school because the teachers couldn't control him. He was a nice boy before the accident but ever since the injuries he has been difficult to control. He needs this money. That is him for life now. What is he going to do without it?'

'I deserve this money and I don't care what anybody says about me,' he said. 'I'm going to buy a big house so I have a place to live with me mum when she gets out of jail. I might buy a few houses – I'll buy whatever I want ... The papers just call me a yob and a thug because I've been done for robbery and assault but those were just silly stupid little things, like.

'I want to spend my money the way I want without people interfering and I want to have a prosperous future. I want to take my mates to Liverpool games and get a flash car. This money is mine now and I'll do what I want. I don't care about anyone or what they have to say about it.'

His plans for the money have no bearing on the case. The money is indeed his and he is entitled to do what he wants with it. Although if he spent it all on cars and football and preferred not to work, then he would again be entitled to relief from public funds. This background has been included only to sway you, the jury.

But some of us can be tempted into hard-hearted argument. He infringed property rights, climbing high on someone else's roof. He courted danger for the many benefits that brings. After his fall, he was treated out of the public purse. He wasn't prosecuted for trespass, or charged for his treatment.

And then he was given half a million pounds because he had been grievously wronged. 'That's him for life.'

As a compensation comparison, the parents of James Bulger received £7,500 after their child was murdered and dumped. The family of Damilola Taylor received £10,000.

Muffin, conkers and Winnie the Pooh

Judging by media coverage, the year 2003 may have been the year that compensation culture peaked. The claims-farming companies hadn't gone bankrupt and compensation claims were getting ever more intense. Things may have levelled off since then. It would be hard to go higher.

This was the year that Muffin the dachshund hurt himself by jumping up for some supermarket leaflets that had been incompletely pushed through the letterbox. Muffin fell awkwardly and hurt himself. The owners came home and found him paralysed from the shoulders down. There were bite marks in the leaflets. They put two and two together. They took him to the vet's, where he underwent an operation (in compensation language, 'a horrendous operation').

The couple were upset. In fact, they were 'devastated' (it's a cruel universe we live in). Two years later, Muffin was still on painkillers, according to the owners (a statement we have to accept). The owners didn't sue for pain or distress. They didn't go on painkillers or anti-depressants themselves.

The party responsible was (obviously) the supermarket that hired the delivery person to push the leaflet through the letterbox.

Mr Musselwhite said Muffin had to be taught to walk again but still could not do so properly and that he sent Safeway a video of Muffin after he had his operation.

Mr Musselwhite claimed £2,300 in vet's bills and legal expenses from Safeway. The ruling went against him. He failed. But, my word, he tried.

⁓

Head teacher Shaun Halfpenny, of Cummersdale Primary School in Carlisle, bought half a dozen pairs of safety goggles for his pupils to protect their eyes when they play conkers in the playground. Pupils queue up at breaks to take turns to use them. Mr Halfpenny said, 'It's just being sensible. We live in a litigious society.'

⁓

Here are some titbits from the annual list from Zurich Municipal.

- A man who tried to sue a local council after he soiled his trousers headed a list of spurious public-liability claims that cost local government and insurance companies (they estimate) £250 million each year.

The man blamed the incident on the council's decision to close a public lavatory at the bus station and argued he was owed the cost of a new pair of trousers.

The list also featured:

- a man who claimed to have injured his arm after slipping on steps owned by a housing association: he had jumped out of his window to avoid being caught with another woman when his girlfriend returned home unexpectedly;

- a bin man who made a claim against his council after being startled by a dead badger that fell out of a bag;

- a shoplifter who sued because she fell downstairs while running from the scene of a crime;

- a motorist who claimed he did not see a traffic roundabout in daylight – despite there being a large tree in the middle.

Iwan Borszcz, claims director for Zurich Municipal, said that while some of the claims were amusing, they caused problems for genuine claimants.

'Whether a claim is exaggerated or completely fraudulent, it is the genuine claimant that suffers,' he said. 'We are constantly amazed at some of the excuses people use to try to claim against public bodies.'

The headlines told us that novelty pig calendars and toys were banned from a council office in case they offend Muslim staff. The report went round the world, and it did wonders for those of us with low blood pressure. It appeared that workers in the benefits department at Dudley Council were told to remove or cover up all pig-related items, including toys, porcelain figures, calendars and even a tissue box featuring Winnie the Pooh and Piglet.

A media myth, surely? Not entirely. The press officer at Dudley admitted the incident happened but she had it confined to one office and to an informal request from one of the Muslim staff, which was complied with by co-workers. It was, she says, never council policy.

It might be noted, in these sensitive times, that the Koran doesn't ban pigs: it just takes a dim view of eating them.

Education, education, compensation!

Freya McDonald, of Moray, settled out of court after suing her education authority, claiming that being put in detention 11 times in nine months at school breached her rights. Her family, who want compensation, argue that the detentions were unlawful because they took place in Freya's free time.

A pupil was expelled from Churston Ferrers Grammar School near Brixham for selling cannabis. The boy failed to get into another school place within six weeks (schools are reluctant to take in teen drug dealers). Torbay Council paid for the child to get five hours of home schooling a week (and later ten hours) against a standard requirement of 25 hours a week. After eight months the boy was placed in a college of further education. The ombudsman ordered the council to pay the family £1,500 to go towards the boy's education and £250 for the father's trouble in chasing up the complaint.

If that juvenile drug dealer is sensitive, he has probably learned a life-changing lesson from this experience. Parents may feel it is not one that the taxpayer should be offering.

Selling drugs in school is now part of the fabric of normal life. You say, 'My son's comprehensive is full of drugs' – and other parents sigh, 'They all are.'

And, considering the official reaction to the drug dealing and its consequences amounting to a cash payment of £1,750, it isn't entirely surprising.

A postman started legal action claiming that he pulled a muscle because there were too many letters in a pillar box. A Wolverhampton postman claimed that George Chryssides, a religious-studies lecturer at the university, owed him compensation for negligently posting about 270 envelopes containing a magazine Chryssides publishes for members of the British Society for the Study of Religions. It weighed around 50 pounds in all and the postman pulled a muscle in his back carrying them, losing £286.96 in pay through time off.

Papers were lodged with Birmingham County Court but the case never got anywhere. Dr Chryssides said at the time, 'Claims of this kind raise the question of whether people can post their Christmas mail without redress.'

The poor fellow is now much more famous as the man who got sued for posting letters than as a doctor of religion. So, if you want any academic advice on the nature of God, please bear him in mind. His book *Unitarian Perspectives on Contemporary Social Issues* is particularly recommended.

~

Bishop Grosseteste College in Lincoln agreed to pay £15,000 compensation and to issue an apology to a disabled member of staff just hours before a disability discrimination case was due to be heard by Nottingham Employment Tribunal. Mrs Sharifa Farley, aged 49, who has the condition of ME (myalgic encephalomyelitis, or chronic-fatigue syndrome) had been part-time disability co-ordinator at the college from 2000. She was sacked in March 2003. No doubt it was prudent to hire a disabled person to be a disability co-ordinator, but this sort of phenomenon is still relatively new in Britain and we can get panicked into hiring people with the wrong sort of disabilities. If you're hiring someone with chronic fatigue to do a part-time job, you probably need two or three of them to complete the same number of hours.

Health-and-safety training leaflets do insist that offices be kept tidy and that drawers be kept shut. Rightly so. Look what happens when they're not.

In January 2006, an insurance worker claimed £5,000 compensation after she tripped and fell over a pile of accident-claim forms. Underwriter Linda Riley reached an out-of-court settlement with Norwich Union's parent company Aviva. Ms Riley, from Newburgh in Fife, claimed that the company was to blame for her tripping over the files, which had been left on the floor.

Her writ claimed, 'The accident was caused through the fault of Aviva. It was its duty to take reasonable care for the safety of its employees and to avoid exposing them to unnecessary risk of injury ... It was its duty to provide her with a safe system of work. It was its duty to ensure there was safe access and egress within the work premises. It was reasonable that if items such as files were left on a traffic route they would present a danger to persons such as Miss Riley. They ought to have known or anticipated an accident would be likely to occur. In each and all of their duties Aviva failed.'

Ms Riley claimed that £5,000 was a fair sum to act as compensation for the loss and injury she suffered as a result of the accident. The level of compensation she accepted was not revealed in court.

Personnel Today

It is this habit of keeping many settlements secret, and of adjudicating cases in chambers that makes it impossible to say with certainty what the level of compensation is in Britain.

Ill wind

A 48-year-old deputy head of a comprehensive school (earning £48,000 a year) made a claim for constructive dismissal, sex discrimination and undue pressure from the management. One of Sue Storer's most persistent tormentors was her nonexecutive chair. 'It was very embarrassing to sit on. I asked for a chair that didn't give me a dead leg or make these very embarrassing farting sounds. It was a regular joke that my chair would make these farting sounds and I regularly had to apologise that it wasn't me, it was my chair.' It's hard enough for teachers to maintain discipline these days, without insolence from the furniture.

Nor was she allocated a new chair when a new consignment arrived. 'I had specially requested a chair under health-and-safety regulations and I didn't get one.' Her health and safety were being compromised daily. She said she had raised the matter with the school's health-and-safety co-ordinator. 'After 12 months of not receiving a chair I put in a memo and still didn't receive one.'

The tribunal was told, however, that one consignment of new chairs sat in reception for two weeks. 'I would have expected her to help herself,' the chairman of the school governors said. Marius Frank, the head teacher, said he would have expected Ms Storer, a member of the school's leadership team, to have had the 'wit and initiative' to sort the problem out. The head teacher showed her a list of complaints about her management practices from colleagues but wouldn't tell her who had said what. As a result, she said she suffered a nervous breakdown and developed severe clinical depression. 'Basically, I wanted to commit suicide. I thought about crashing my car.'

Her claim of £1 million was based on lost earnings and lost pension. This amounts to full cash payment for the rest of her working life.

The initial story made all the front pages; however, the verdict made the third news-in-brief item halfway down page 25 of *The Times*. The judges ignored the fact that she had wanted to commit suicide, that she had thought about crashing her car and that only the application of £1 million to her personal circumstances would properly compensate her for the emotional roller coaster she'd been subjected to. They dismissed her claims, in short, and told her she should have got her own chair.

Some will say this proves a compensation culture doesn't exist; others will say it would have been impossible to think about bringing such a case in front of a tribunal unless a compensation culture was firmly in place.

Officials told Lord Bingham (senior Law Lord) that bookshelves in the proposed Supreme Court library could not be placed above shoulder height. Why not? Someone might fall and hurt themselves if books could not be taken off the shelves without the use of a chair or a ladder. Lord Bingham reportedly said, 'This has to be the stupidest regulation that anybody has ever made.'

Not now, darling!

Workers at the English National Opera have been banned from using the term of endearment 'darling' to each other. The policy, set out in a document called 'Dignity at Work', singles out the word 'darling' as part of a code of conduct that addresses workplace protocol. It tells employees, 'The use of affectionate names such as "darling" may constitute sexual harassment.' A grievance procedure is available for those who are made uncomfortable by hearing the word. The policy is still in place. It all seems perfectly normal to the administration there. It's the way we live now.

A dyslexic banker named Robert but nicknamed 'Trebor' by his boss – his first name spelt backwards – was awarded damages of £95,000 by an employment tribunal. Robert Huskisson claimed that the taunting he received from colleagues at Abbey National reminded him of the bullying he endured as a schoolboy from other pupils who considered him stupid because of his condition.

Instead of giving him support, he said, his superiors ended up dismissing him for failing to meet sales targets.

After a hearing before the tribunal in Ashford, Kent, in 2001, Mr Huskisson won his case for disability discrimination. It appears from the report (in the *Telegraph*) that he was fired less because of his disability and more because he failed to reach sales targets.

Thus, the £95,000 compensation seems to have been awarded because people were rude to him. He described it as 'a pretty good amount but a lot less than we hoped for'.

An aside from a solicitor's newsletter:

'An area of potentially valid claims concerns the failure of an educational establishment to note the signs of dyslexia in a pupil and refer that pupil to an educational psychologist. One of our education clients was therefore somewhat taken aback to be asked to pay a claim for compensation arising from the stigmatisation of a pupil who had been so referred but where the educational psychologist had rejected dyslexia as a diagnosis.' (From Berrymans Lace Mawer, solicitors.)

Accidents Won't Happen

'I feel very strongly that individuals should not be restrained from carrying on sporting activities that involve risk, like hang-gliding or swimming.'

Lord Phillips, the Law Lord responsible
for the civil courts in England and Wales

The safety principle many middle-aged people were brought up with can be summarised as, 'Well, you won't do that again.' Child presents itself with cuts, bruises, wobbly knees. Responsible adult gives it a hug (can't do that any more, either) and sends it along with the important phrase ringing in its ears. The principle of learning from experience is no longer on the curriculum, and the concept of an accident as a random act of bad luck is under steady pressure from a variety of interests – certainly from claims farmers.

For instance, an Accident Line leaflet called 'It was Just an Accident – or was it?' sets about drumming up business by saying 'many people who believed at first that their accident could not be blamed on anyone but themselves have gone on to make successful claims'.

A *British Medical Journal* editorial in 2001 argued against the concept of anything called an 'accident', saying that most undesirable events are preventable and that 'injuries of all kinds' can be predicted and therefore prevented ('all kinds'!). This is barking mad for many of us, but we have to try to stay in contact with the world as it is.

The *BMJ* editorial went on to ask whether injuries received in an earthquake or other natural disaster could be called accidental since 'preventive steps can be taken by avoiding dangerous places at times of risk'. It recommended that the emergency medicine establishment in the UK 'will jettison "accidents" as have its counterparts in the US, Canada and many other countries'. For its own part, the *BMJ* would 'ban the word accident' from its pages.

There has been a swing back towards the side of sanity in a number of (we might hope) landmark decisions (see Pages 202–209), but there's quite a way to go as these six cases show (they were presented by the Parliamentary All-Party Group on Adventure and Recreation in Society to the Constitutional Affairs Committee).

1. The slippery slope (1)

'A Scout campsite had created a water slide on a gentle slope, by laying a length of heavy-duty polythene on the ground which was then covered with soapy water. The supervising adults explained that people should not run and dive onto the sheet but that they should simply sit at the top. For safety, the participants were provided with lightweight, plastic canoeing helmets and were instructed to fasten these securely before descending. A youth leader with a party of non-scout children decided to have a go. He selected a helmet without reference to the supervising Scout Leaders (who were checking that the helmets were secure) and dived headlong down the slope. The loosely fitted helmet struck the ground and the front slipped down cutting the bridge of his nose. This was a relatively minor injury. However, a claim was brought and the matter proceeded to trial. The Scouts lost and the Judge held that the Scout Leaders should have ensured that people could not get on to the slide without the helmets being checked.'

Joseph Morrison v. *The Scout Association*; date of accident, 8 August 2000; litigation commenced 6 September 2000, judgment given by HH Judge Brownlee at Newtownards, 6 November 2002

This tells us that even youth supervisors need supervising. But who will supervise the supervisors' supervisors? How could that Scout leader have been allowed into a position to let another adult put himself in such a dangerous position? The convicted Scout leader, in fact, almost certainly has a claim against his superiors in the organisation: they allowed him into an unsafe environment without adequate training. And why weren't those superiors alerted to the risks of their recklessness? Whom can they sue? The Health and Safety Executive, perhaps? For failing to enforce suitable training protocols on the supervisors' supervising supervisors?

2. Sailor beware!

'The skipper of a lightweight 25ft racing yacht was successfully sued by one of the experienced crew members after manoeuvring to leave a marina. The skipper, realising that the yacht had been caught by a gust of wind and might hit an adjacent moored yacht, asked an experienced adult crew member to run forward with a fender. The crew member stumbled going forward and three months later successfully sued the skipper for damages claiming he had injured his leg. After a five-day trial the Court found the skipper liable on the grounds that a reasonably careful skipper should have pre-briefed the crew on this manoeuvre and had a crew member pre-placed.

'The sailing fraternity was amazed at this decision as sailing is a rough-and-tumble sport and experienced crew are frequently asked to hurry forward or aft to deal with an emergency. It is up to the crew member to decide whether to obey the skipper on grounds of safety and how best to carry out that instruction.'

Richards v. *Wanstall*; High Court, Queen's Bench Division,
Admiralty Division, 10 April 1995

3. Dangerous waters

'At the British Canoe Union [BCU] Marathon in 2004, crews were competing over a 30-mile course in racing kayaks. Part of the course passed through a narrow, half-mile long cutting. A volunteer marshal was positioned at each end of the cutting to warn crews entering it about any powered craft which could present a danger. A power boat entered the cutting and four minutes later a kayak arrived at the cutting travelling in the same direction. The marshal allowed it to enter on the strict understanding that there was a powered craft in the cutting and that they should not try to overtake it. The kayak crew ignored the instruction and overtook the boat causing damage to it.

'A claim was made against the volunteer marshal alleging he should have assumed the crew would have ignored his instruction and he was therefore negligent.

'The claim was settled via the BCU insurance after taking legal advice, but the race organisers now face increased insurance costs and the volunteer will not be offering his services again.'

The case was settled out of court.

Question: Realising that his warning might be ignored, to what lengths should the marshal have gone to prevent the canoe entering the cutting? Should he have jumped into the water, grabbed the back of the canoe, and forcibly restrained them?

And, if you think the question facetious, consider this next case.

4. The Gaping Ghyll incident

'A Scout Group had organised a trip to visit the popular show cave at Gaping Ghyll in Yorkshire. Some parents had gone along as additional supervising adults.

'The party decided to eat their picnic lunch before undertaking the guided tour and walked a short distance up a footpath to some open land. One of the Scouts [called Craddock] noticed a small cave opening across a stream and asked the Scout Leader for permission to explore it. The Leader refused permission, pointing out that caves could be dangerous. The Scout then moved away to where his father stood and repeated the request. His father, who had heard the leader's ruling, gave permission, provided his son with a cigarette lighter for illumination and accompanied him into the cave. A short distance inside, the Scout slipped and fell down a "chimney" leading into the main chamber of Gaping Ghyll. He fell 300 feet to his death.

'The father sued the Scout Association. The judge found in favour of the claimant, stating that, as he was born in a city, he could not have been expected to recognise the dangers. He held that the Scout Leader should have prevented the father from entering the cave, by force if necessary, and in failing to do so he breached his duty of care.

'The Craddocks' older son continued as a member of the same Group for two years after the accident leaving when he reached 18 with his Chief Scout Award. The litigation did not commence until after he left.'

The Gaping Ghyll Incident. *Craddock* v. *(1) Dr J A Farrer, (2) The Scout Association*; date of Accident 25 July 1995; litigation commenced 23 July 1998, judgment given by H H Judge Appleton in Preston, 17 November 2000

Question: if the Scout Leader had laid hands on the parent, wouldn't he have been guilty of assault? A further question: are city people now considered disabled by their metropolitan experience of life? In which case, shouldn't they be given training to go into the countryside? City-born ramblers surely ought to do a course and pass a test for a Certificate of Rural Competence and carry an annually renewable licence to be carried for inspection by Ramblers' Marshals (who should have powers of detention). Maybe Rural Competence can be a new category on their identity card when they come in.

5. Height of dismay

'A professional mountain guide was held liable for the death of his fellow climber because he failed to take adequate safety precautions when proceeding with a manoeuvre. This was not based on any dispute about facts. It was based on the judge's decision that he believed the mountain guide underestimated the potential danger posed by a rock fall in a split second decision taken on the mountain face. The decision was received with considerable dismay in the worlds of mountain/rock climbing and other inherently dangerous sports.'

Hedley v. *Cuthbertson*, Queen's Bench Division, Dyson J, 20 June 1997

6. The slippery slope (2)

'Six years ago Woodbridge School permitted three senior boys to join junior pupils on a ski trip. It did so on terms agreed with parents and purely as a favour to the three boys. The boys, while under overall control of the supervising teacher and his colleagues as to their conduct on the trip, were to be permitted to ski unsupervised on all the slopes at Kuhtai and, as they were older than the other pupils, were to be treated as such. But they were to remember they were representatives of the school and expected to behave as such.

'The parents agreed to these conditions. Simon Paul Chittock, one of the 16-year-old senior boys on the school trip, behaved so badly on the ski slope that he had to be repeatedly reproved by the teachers who were giving their time to escort him. Twice he skied off-piste. Finally he had a serious accident and broke his back. The parents sued the school and won the case in the lower courts on the grounds that their son should have been prevented from skiing once he proved to be irresponsible. This would have meant either leaving him unsupervised in the resort or an instructor staying with him, denying other youngsters the opportunity to ski.

'This case was overturned on Appeal but not because the higher court denied the premise that Chittock should have been left at the hotel. The grounds for the appeal were that he was on-piste, skiing normally when the accident happened.'

Woodbridge School v. *Simon Paul Chittock*; original hearing by Judge Leveson, 25 July 2001; Appeal Court hearing 13–14 June 2002

Note: The child's parents sued because their son was a pain in the arse. He'd had an accident and the parents found it impossible to comprehend that their son could be hurt without someone else being to blame for it.

Derek Twine (chief executive of the Scout Association) said that they had undertaken an internal survey and found 50 per cent of volunteers were affected by the threat of being sued for compensation. And that 70 per cent testified that the fear of being sued was a deterrent to recruiting additional volunteers.

The All-Party Group made the surprising claim that many Sea Cadets no longer sail on the sea:

'Instructors continue to lose cases, as the courts have repeatedly produced unfair findings of negligence, especially where young people have been allowed to take responsibility for themselves and suffered or caused accidents.

'Today 80,000 youngsters are on waiting lists for the Scouts and Guides alone.'

Why is there such a waiting list? There aren't enough instructors. And why aren't there enough instructors?

'Fear of litigation is the top barrier to volunteering. The Scouts and Guides make the point, however, that it is not just about rising insurance premia, dire as those are; a scoutmaster who is accused by lawyers in court of being incompetent is very unlikely to return to scouting even if he wins.'

It's the parents, isn't it? They're the ones suing. Perhaps they think it would be immoral not to sue, since the money is there for the taking. And because everyone else is doing it. Why shouldn't they? The answer should be sought from those 80,000 youngsters on waiting lists for the Scouts and Guides.

Post-traumatic Public Servants

A soldier recently received £377,000 after alleging that the army failed to protect him from frostbite while he was on exercises in Canada. Another received £387,000 for 'negligent treatment of warts'.

～

An Aberdeen police dog handler launched a £15,000 claim against Grampian police, claiming Alsatians' barking had made him deaf. He settled out of court, according to *Noise & Vibration Worldwide*, 1 April 2001.

～

As we've noted in Chapter 1, Jamie Bulger's parents received £7,500 from the Criminal Injuries Compensation Board (now Criminal Injuries Compensation Authority) after he was murdered. A police press officer dealing with media enquiries about the case had a terrible time, too, she said. She claimed compensation in the region of (it was suggested at the time) £100,000 because senior officers in Merseyside Police hadn't helped her cope with the deluge of media enquiries following the murder. When she was passed over for promotion, she quit and started an action against the police. She dropped the case shortly before it was due in court.

～

Two police officers sought £400,000 each for attending the scene of the Dunblane school shootings in March 1996 and for 'not receiving proper stress counselling'.

～

Phil Hammond lost a 14-year-old son in the crush of the Hillsborough Stadium disaster of 1989. He received £3,500 compensation.

Nine years after the disaster, a former police sergeant who developed symptoms of post-traumatic stress disorder was awarded more than £300,000. Also, 14 other police officers accepted a total settlement of £1.2 million. Mr Hammond called the payment to the police officer 'disgusting', adding, 'There are people who lost their sons, daughters and loved ones and received nothing. There is a huge difference between the amount paid to the police and the amount paid to survivors.'

It is worth remembering, as an aside, that the disaster was caused by the police themselves. Lord Justice

Taylor's official inquiry into the disaster was quite clear: 'The real cause of the Hillsborough disaster [was] overcrowding, the main reason for the disaster was the failure of police control.'

The Lords of Appeal ruled on this, saying, 'So far as rescue was concerned, police officers must be regarded as professional rescuers. They will not be persons of ordinary phlegm, but of extraordinary phlegm hardened to events which would to ordinary persons cause distress.' (*White and others* v. *Chief Constable of North Yorkshire*).

Blood money

Early in 2006, six prison warders shared around £1 million in damages and legal costs for 'severe psychological injuries' suffered five years earlier.

They had responded to an emergency buzzer from a cell. They opened the door and saw what their solicitor called, without overstatement, a scene of 'Gothic horror'. The living occupant of the cell, Jason Ricketts, had murdered his cellmate, Colin Bloomfield, by cutting open his stomach and removing his liver, which he placed on a chair. He had also removed an eyeball. 'I was going to eat his heart,' the killer is reported to have said. The prison officers ended up in the dead man's blood, and one of them tried, hopelessly, to resuscitate the corpse. Gruesome business.

But what was the money for? Was it to punish the Home Office (so they'd improve their systems) or to compensate the officers?

And what is a manager to do? When your officers' hands are on the doorknob and they know something terrible is on the other side of the door, what do you, as their manager, do? Do you tell them to go in? And, if they don't go in, who does? Whose job is it to clear up after disasters? And does the clean-up always take a tariff of £200,000 per person?

And how much would the cellmate have been entitled to, had he lived? Almost certainly much less than £200,000, according to the tariff. He would have got much less than those forced to witness the mess he had become.

~~

A speeding policeman (travelling 'much too fast', according to the judge) had a crash for which he was 50 per cent responsible. The civilian's wife, in the other car, was killed. The policeman, George Gilfillan, received £87,000 for the post-traumatic stress of seeing her die. The surviving husband received £16,000. The case was heard in the Court of Session in Edinburgh.

Gone walkabout

Primary school teacher Jan Howell was in 1999 awarded £254,000 in compensation after showing that her job had driven her towards a nervous breakdown.

A sympathetic account of her travails comes from www.bullyonline.org:

'The head teacher ignored Jan Howell's calls for help on a number of occasions. The final straw came when the disturbed youngster absconded from her class during the morning session and was seen walking along the edge of the tidal part of the adjacent river which contains dangerous mud flats. Jan Howell was beside herself with worry. She had asked to be informed if the boy's mother telephoned to say he had arrived home safely. She was not informed until the end of the day. The head teacher had forgotten to relay the information despite being told at midday. It was then that Jan Howell experienced her second breakdown. She never returned to work.'

Let's show a moment's lack of compassion. To allow yourself to be driven to a nervous breakdown because some stupid child insists on walking on a riverbank may be a symptom of extreme hypersensitivity. It suggests a spirit too fine for the coarseness of the world. A quarter of a million pounds (that is, ten years' salary) can hardly have helped such a delicate nature.

But it's not all a one-way business. Sometimes compensation turns and turns about.

In 2003, a former prison officer saw that one of his former inmates had received the sum of £75,000 from his local authority. They had failed to provide a suitable education. Because they hadn't given him a place in a boarding school the boy had gone off the rails and into a life of crime, his lawyers argued.

The prison officer, Malcolm Joyce, was particularly annoyed because the offender, Marvin Pomfret, had been the inmate who'd held him hostage for 20 hours, blindfolded him, gagged him, repeatedly slashed him about the face, battered him with a baseball bat, threatened to kill him, and removed the blindfold so he could see darts being thrown at him. Pomfret and his collaborators had threatened to cut off his fingers and post them through the window.

Mr Joyce said, 'I felt that any such money should have gone first to his victims and thereafter, if any was left, to charity. If that had happened I would never have gone to litigation.'

By that time, most of the £75,000 had been swallowed in lawyers' fees. Out of the remaining £20,000, Marvin had given half to his girlfriend, so the prison officer was awarded about a third of what was left.

In the line of duty

In 2000, a local government officer and sometime gypsy, Randy Ingram, won £203,000 after his life was 'ruined' by work as a gipsy site manager for Worcester City Council. 'The council has a lot to answer for,' Mr Ingram said. 'They have made me very ill with stress and depression and my home life has suffered as a result.' As he had been shot at, and physically and verbally abused by gypsies on the sites where he worked, it wasn't entirely the council's fault. The gypsies (his sometime neighbours and ethnic colleagues) had something to do with it, what with the guns and abuse.

‑‑

'Many of the issues affecting employers, such as harassment, discrimination legislation, and so on also affect the army and police services. However, claims have now been made concerning issues that were traditionally seen as part of the norm in the "line of duty". For example, the army has been sued by a soldier who has claimed for the stress of seeing his colleague killed on duty.'

The above is from www.actuaries.org.uk.

General Sir Charles Guthrie said, 'But what really concerns me about the creeping advance of litigation is that it will breed a cautious group of leaders who may step back from courageous decisions for fear that they will be pursued through the courts if it all goes wrong.

'There is a culture of risk aversion developing in society which is anathema to servicemen. We are not foolhardy but our profession requires a degree of decisiveness, flair and courage which sits badly with some of the more restrictive practices of modern employment legislation.'

In particular, General Guthrie attacked the idea recently floated by figures within British officialdom that the military should be compelled to accept disabled recruits: 'We need to guard against such ill-conceived ideas in future.'

The Happiest Days of Our Lives

We're all very sensitive about our children lately, I don't know why. It's hard to take any other line on the glutinous displays of parental piety we see at the school gates these days.

When those Australian gold miners (trapped half a mile underground in a cage for nearly a week in May 2006) were first contacted through a tiny hole in the rubble, practically the first thing they asked for was a newspaper so they could look for another job. One of the mothers said, 'Todd's putting in for meal allowance, overtime pay and living-away-from-home allowance, so I hope they've got their chequebook ready.'

That's what I want my children to grow up like!

'My wife was at work when she received the chilling call from the nursery: our two-year-old son Jim had had an accident,' writes Ian Evans in *The Times* of 31 January 2006. 'She grabbed her bag and keys, ready to drive to the nearest hospital. In fact he'd only grazed his knee; the nursery nurse was seeking permission to put a plaster on, then passed the phone to her supervisor to confirm that the OK had been given. A one-off, you might think, but in fact this is not untypical in the all-caring, all-smothering – and paranoid – world of nursery schools.'

And from the same article:

- Emma Bracewell, in Suffolk, was told not to bring in egg boxes to her sons' nursery. 'They said it was because of fears over salmonella – from the boxes.'
- Kiran Jones, in Bromley, southeast London, discovered that his nursery wouldn't administer Calpol to his nine-month-old because he hadn't left a spoon.
- Laurent Lucas, a former nursery worker, explains: 'We live in a society where people often sue for "negligence". I have had parents complaining because their child had an allergic reaction to a plaster.'

~

'There is such a terror of litigation that the number of independent schools offering rugby has fallen by 30 per cent over the past 15 years,' writes Boris Johnson.

Too much sun

Guidelines issued by the Derby City Council tell teachers who plan to lead students on summer trips that they should consider keeping a supply of maximum-factor sun cream to spray onto pupils, although they should not rub it in for fear of being accused of inappropriate contact.

In Bristol, staff at Hillcrest Primary school confiscated a bottle of Factor 60 sunblock that an eight-year-old boy had brought to school, because it was forbidden for students to possess medication, according to the BBC News website. If the child was easily sunburned, he should have worn a long-sleeved shirt and sun hat. Offering the simplest solution to safety problems, the council suggested that educators consider cancelling field outings entirely on days that are too sunny.

Bonkers!

A survey in 2000 by Keele University researcher Sarah Thomson showed that some schools have banned conkers because they fear the horse chestnuts could be used as 'offensive weapons'. She said, 'I even heard one member of staff talk about banning conkers because she linked conkers with nuts, which might then expose children to nut allergies.'

This is only partially a safety question. If the possibility didn't exist that parents might sue when their nut-allergic children were exposed to conkers, then we would all take a more robust attitude to infinitesimal risks.

Other schools banned football on the grounds that it is antisocial, while another banned skipping after some girls fell over. Ms Thomson said that the lunch break was in danger of becoming 'a sterile, joyless time as schools over-react to an increasingly litigious society'. She has been keeping an eye on the trend regarding schools and their fear of litigation, and she said this: 'I think that some schools are still very sensitive to parental litigation (although some are aware of the failure of many parents to successfully pursue a claim for compensation as far as injuries in the playground are concerned).

'Schools often settle out of court because they are afraid of the bad publicity and negative media coverage, therefore admitting liability rather than defending themselves publicly. This tends to reinforce the myth that schools are at fault rather than [their] visibly refuting (and sometimes winning the claim) and deterring other claimants.

'I found that the schools I visited all had had a/some parents attempting to sue them for negligence or injury to their child at playtime or in the school building, but when the LEA legal team started to construct a defence, that is by visiting the school, viewing the scene of the accident and taking statements from the staff (all very stressful of course for the school) often they either found that the school was not negligent and advised the head accordingly or the parent was warned off by the fact that that their accusation was being taken seriously and that they might not have a case anyway.

'I think overall (very generally) schools have become more cautious with regards to playtime injuries. Schools are also driven by HSE requirements and this also tends to make them cautious. This combined with OFSTED and the litigation environment tends to make them want to cover every aspect of child safety and damage limitation. I think there is an overall hypersensitivity towards children's playtime safety/safety.

'I have just heard of a boy (secondary school level) being suspended for three days for throwing a snowball!'

Dr Sarah Thomson (Keele University)

The banned played on

A health-and-safety risk assessment that was ordered by Wiltshire County Council led Abbeyfield, the secondary school in Chippenham, to ban footballs from the playground.

One of the pupils said, 'Everyone used to play a lot of football, but now they don't. The rule change has really discouraged people. You can't play touch rugby on the fields because they are "too wet" and you can't play on the hard court because that's dangerous. So now no one plays touch rugby any more either. Lots of people just play with bouncy balls, but I suspect that'll be banned too before too long.'

One of the girl pupils said, 'I think this football ban is stupid. People are used to playing football, and when they come to Abbeyfield they can't. Now we play with bottles. I probably play twice or three times a week with empty Coke bottles, but it's not nearly as fun.'

Tim Perry, the deputy head, insisted that students are still allowed to play contact sports, but only in 'supervised environments'. He denied that the school was in danger of fostering a 'namby-pamby attitude'.

But here's the question that would (if answered in the right way) reverse the entire set of decisions. Wouldn't a longer-term health-and-safety risk assessment reveal that obesity caused by lack of exercise would be significantly more dangerous and produce inexorably more illness and death than that caused by any schoolyard football?

The *Sunday Telegraph* sent out a questionnaire to 30 schools and found the following.

- Harbinger Primary School in Tower Hamlets: conkers banned. Throwing snowballs banned.

- Abbeyfield: playground football banned. Unsupervised contact sports banned.

- Maney Hill Primary School, Sutton Coldfield: conkers banned.

- Sayers Court School, Surrey: tag banned. British Bulldogs banned.

- Upton School, the Wirral: rubber bracelet in gym banned ('too dangerous for certain types of activity').

- St Anne's Primary, Denton, Greater Manchester: pencil cases banned (a pupil had been harmed by a letter opener smuggled into school in a pencil case).

- Crudwell Church of England Primary school banned fairy cakes at their school summer fête, allowing only shop-bought ones (risk assessment: food poisoning).

- Killigrew Junior School, St Albans: swimming goggles banned (elastic straps could snap back and hit children in the face).

The feeding of grass pellets to goats has been banned according to some, or discouraged according to others, at the farm at Wimpole Hall, the National Trust property in Cambridgeshire, for fear that young visitors will pick up diseases and germs.

'We have not imposed a ban as such,' a National Trust spokesman said. 'What we have done is withdrawn the invitation for visitors to handle eggs after they have been laid or to feed grass pellets to the goats.'

The deciding factor was not that any illnesses had been reported by the 120,000 people who visit Home Farm every year since 1983, but the advice of the Health Protection Agency.

Again – and we'll return to this important theme – this isn't primarily a health issue but one of compensation. People simply wouldn't bother with this sort of ban if they didn't feel the risk of litigation hanging over them.

From the minutes of an ordinary meeting of Halberton (Devon) Parish Council, 12 October 2004, concerning the recreation ground.

'Cllr Lane-Smith explained that a MDDC approved play equipment supplier had visited the site to provide quotes for new equipment. However the supplier had indicated that the play surface was non-compliant and didn't meet safety standards and the Rec' should be closed with immediate effect. Cllr Lane-Smith had also been advised by an Officer at MDDC that the current play area surface was unsuitable. The Chairman advised that the site was checked annually by Rospa [Royal Society for the Prevention of Accidents, usually styled RoSPA] who had found the surface to meet safety standards. The last time it was inspected was in March 2004 when the current surfacing was in situ. Rospa was a well respected organisation and therefore the Chairman considered that there was an over-reaction by the PC if the site was to close immediately. There was much discussion followed by the following resolution: The playground to remain open for 24 hours during which time the Clerk to obtain advice from the Health and Safety Executive and Rospa. A decision would be made after the advice had been obtained. If the Rec' was to close, signs to be erected on gates and equipment prohibiting use and the gates to be locked. The Vice-Chairman to obtain quotes for safety fencing. In addition the Clerk to obtain a certificate of compliance from the supplier of the surfacing.'

Doctor, Doctor, I've Got a Pain

'Malingering has its origins in the military and only became medicalised with the development of the welfare state and workmen's compensation schemes at the beginning of the 20th century.'

Malingering and Illness Deception, Peter Halligan, Chris Bass, David Oakley, Oxford University Press, 2003

'How confident is he that the measures that he has announced today will put an end to the overtime scams, the sickness scams and the early-retirement scams that tarnish the reputation of British police?'

Chris Mullin MP, 2001, House of Commons question to the Home Secretary

I had an email from a regional chief constable after an article I'd done about the government way with statistics. The minister had been celebrating the increase in police funding. This chief constable told me that every penny of his extra budget was going on the pensions of officers who were taking early retirement.

In 2003, we had the case of a policeman from Greater Manchester going on long-term sick leave (the now-traditional 'bad back'), during which time he started a new career as a parachute instructor. Another officer of 22 years' standing launched a claim for damages against the police, alleging that his back was injured when he slipped on a wet floor at Bury police station. He resigned when it was revealed that he had made up the incident. In December 2004, two traffic policemen from the same force were ordered to hand back £35,000. They had made £83,000 by moonlighting as private safety consultants.

Police officers are entitled to six months off sick on full pay in any one year, followed by half-pay for the remaining six months.

We don't know how many thousands of police officers are receiving full pay for as little as one hour's work a day. They are on 'restricted duties' following long-term illness or depression. They are paid their full salary (around £30,000) irrespective of the hours they work. In September 2005, Metropolitan Commissioner Sir Ian Blair revealed that 2,000 such officers in London alone are picking up their entire salaries. If the same level of compensation is being paid to police nationwide (and no one knows because such statistics aren't collected centrally), this practice carries a cost of £300 million.

A 27-year-old 'bad-back' shelf stacker, Andrew Perry, underwent hospital treatment, including spinal injections, and sued his employer for negligence, according to the *This Is London* online news source. His employers, Makro's, hadn't taught him how to lift things, and as a result he'd never be able to do physically demanding work again, he claimed. Makro's were preparing to pay out £200,000 in compensation when they received a photograph from Andrew Perry's ex-girlfriend showing him jet-skiing and doing somersault dives into a Majorcan swimming pool.

'You caught me on a good day' is the normal defence in these circumstances, but Mr Perry dropped his case because it was difficult to prove whether these injuries were the result of shelf stacking or jet-skiing. 'I didn't want to waste taxpayers' money,' he said (confused, as he might be, about the source of money).

Makro's detectives found that Mr Perry had been plotting an accident before his claim went in.

Interestingly, he was prepared to undergo spinal injections to support his claim. Mind you, £200,000 is a powerful incentive to damage yourself.

A car worker, Brian Murphy, went off on sick leave and set up his own business doing handyman/gardening work. Nissan found out (his ad for work appeared by mistake on their website). They dismissed him. He sued for wrongful dismissal and won £65,000 compensation because the company policy did not explicitly forbid staff taking temporary paid work when ill.

An employment tribunal in Newcastle upon Tyne found that Mr Murphy, a paint-shop team leader, had not breached company rules by setting up a handyman business while off with a stress-related illness.

Murphy, who had worked at the Sunderland plant for 16 years, was sacked after being filmed laying a lawn and mending a fence by a private detective.

～

Not much research has been done into medical benefit fraud. But in Britain doctors issue around 22 million sick notes a year, of which 9 million are thought by the Norwich Union insurance firm to be questionable. The Confederation of British Industry puts it a little lower at around 7 million.

'A lack of ability to confront patients is a deficiency in GPs' skills. The epidemic of illness behaviour and sick role adoption is partly our fault,' said G.Mackenzie, in the *British Medical Journal* in 2004.

The orthodoxy among doctors is that fraud is rare. This is the opinion of people whose entire professional training has been based on the generous practice of believing what their patients say. Doctors don't go into medicine to act as state gatekeepers to the benefit system. They are not the work police. They become doctors to make people better, to treat people, to alleviate symptoms. A good, sincere, professional doctor is the easiest person in Britain to deceive.

But when the doctor doesn't play ball there can be severe consequences.

And this situation isn't new. As far back as nearly 30 years ago a patient diagnosed as malingering by four orthopaedic surgeons shot three (killing two) before taking his own life, according to *Medical Journal Australia* in 1979. One of the doctors had written, 'I can only say that if he has a real disability it is buried under such a mass of functional disorder that I cannot discern it.'

Depressing news

The British journalist Matthew Parris found an alarming level of dependency on antidepressants on a number of housing estates in the northeast of England. The drugs had become fashionable. Young mothers would demand the drugs from their doctor. If the doctor put up an honourable resistance he or she would be defeated by an unanswerable argument: 'If you don't give me the drugs, I can't answer for what I'd do to the kids.' It is entirely conceivable that such a mother might hurt her children in order to prove her point. 'I told them. I warned them. They didn't listen.'

Once you are on antidepressants, it's very difficult to get off them; and, of course, there is no possibility of your being forced to work, if you are on the treatment. Antidepressants form a vital part of the compensation evidence. If you're serious about a claim for any long-term psychological damage, it is essential you've seen the doctor for antidepressants. You can show that you have been prescribed them without even lying (you don't, after all, have to take them).

~

A firm of lawyers, Higgins and Co., from Birkenhead in the Wirral, was offering GPs £175 for every patient referred to them. The British Medical Association's view was that doctors shouldn't be offered money for compensation referrals. The practice was 'inappropriate and gives the appearance of a conflict of interest'. For instance, in cases of unclear diagnosis doctors would have an incentive to diagnose an ailment for which compensation could be sought rather than one for which there is no one to blame.

~

Objective research in such a subjective and political area as compensation is rare. Maybe it doesn't exist. You could produce research to prove almost any point. The TUC will say that workers are vastly undercompensated (that 90 per cent of accident victims receive nothing).

But, then again, why should sickness-benefit claims be given the benefit of our generous credulity? Why should sickness claimants be any more honest and honourable than the rest of us? Endless studies show we're all less scrupulous, less honest than we used to be: in 2002, academics Mitchell and Chan found that

- more than 77 per cent of shoppers claim not to have owned up to getting too much change;
- 40 per cent of shoppers have walked out without paying for goods;
- 77 per cent have lied about a child's age to get a reduced price.

In Matthew Wynia's famous American survey, 54 per cent of respondents admitted to deceiving insurers. That wouldn't be a surprising result if the respondents were scroungers, malingerers and conmen – but they were doctors. Fifty-four per cent of US physicians in the sample admitted to something like fraud. And 85 per cent of doctors believed it was unethical to 'use the system for your patient's benefit' (including a majority of those who admitted doing it themselves).

Lawyers were as bad, probably worse. I don't know why I say 'probably'. Lawyers are known to coach the patients (or clients, as they have become) to get them through the insurer's medical examination. They advise how to respond to psychological tests; they would make suggestion of what to tell the examining psychologist and what to emphasise, and would warn clients not to disclose certain information important to psychologists (see Page 133 for some very detailed coaching).

If you resist the idea that faking, skiving and malingering is a venerable and active part of our national character, consider this whiplash fact:

British whiplash neck injuries account for 85 per cent of all motor-accident personal-injury claims in UK. But three studies have shown that, in those countries where compensation is not available after a crash, whiplash almost never occurs.

NB: Whiplash is a sprain. It lasts two weeks at the most. If neck pain lasts any longer, it's not whiplash.

~~

Has occupational ill health increased? The numbers of occupational cases may have gone up but then again, there are 5 million more people in work now. Health has improved by almost every indicator you can think of, but the number of people claiming incapacity benefit has increased almost as dramatically as the number of people claiming compensation. Odd, that. Professor Gordon Waddell (in *The Scientific and Conceptual Basis of Incapacity Benefits*) suggests that 70 per cent of incapacity-benefit (IB) recipients don't have the symptoms to explain their disability in medical terms.

The number of IB recipients has more than trebled since 1979 to 2.7 million. Quite a large proportion of them were encouraged off the unemployment roll and onto the sick list in order to improve the statistics for Mrs Thatcher's restructuring programme. Perhaps for that reason, a million of these claimants say they want to return to work.

But what's the total of people malingering on public funds? Again, an impossible number to calculate accurately. The total incapacity benefit in 1998 was £12 billion. The prime minister thinks 30 per cent of incapacity beneficiaries should get back to work. As do a third of claimants themselves.

There is a lot of culture in compensation. In parts of Wales 25 per cent of males are on incapacity benefit. In the Home Counties the rate is 3 per cent. There are no medical explanations, only cultural ones.

'What seems to have happened is that the employment threshold has gradually moved down the severity scale, so that men and women with middle-severity impairments who would have been employed in the 1970s are now out of work and receiving incapacity benefits,' according to *Disability Benefits: A review of the issues and options for reform*, by Richard Berthoud.

The rate of ill-heath retirement among workers on the state payroll is a third higher than in the private sector. Sixty-eight per cent of all firefighters who retired did so on the grounds of ill health. In the police, 49 per cent of early retirement is due to ill health.

Lord Dixon-Smith asked Her Majesty's Government: How many man-years of service are currently unavailable due to police officers taking early retirement; and what are the comparable figures for 1996 and 1991.

Lord Rooker: These figures are not centrally available.

The government Department for Work and Pensions has said the level of benefit fraud in Britain is £3 billion but that was a figure it plucked out of the air. The way the National Audit Office phrased this admission went like this: 'Because of the nature of the Department's estimates, based on rolling programmes that produce estimates subject to statistical uncertainties and snap-shot reviews that are up to six years old, the £3 billion is not a precise figure but is the best estimate available at present.'

Here is an extract from Hansard:

'Mr Paul Goodman (Wycombe) (Con): I begin my speech in this important debate by briefly telling the story of Martin Crowson. Mr Crowson, who is from Manchester, said that he was virtually unable to walk. On that basis, he made a claim and was paid more than £17,000 in incapacity benefits. Last May, it was reported that Mr Crowson had been sentenced and jailed by a Manchester court after certificates were unearthed that confirmed that while he was receiving his £17,000 of taxpayers' money on the basis of his apparent incapacity, he was also training for a black belt in judo. Photographs of Mr Crowson also came to light in which he was posed riding a camel and wrestling with an alligator.

'The Secretary of State for Work and Pensions (Mr David Blunkett): That is the new test.'

Scouse scams

How much fraud is there in the system?

It's very hard drawing any conclusion from statistics that have been compiled to conceal the truth. You can, however, get a sense of how little trust you should place in official statistics. Try this for a commonsense test.

Liverpool City Council got a very good report from the fraud inspectors. The inspectors said that the council had 'a credible and high-profile counter-fraud service and this was demonstrated by its application of the full range of sanctions available'. So then, what would that result in? In terms of prosecutions for fraudulent benefit claims? In Liverpool, the most resourceful, energetic and ingenious city in Britain – possibly the Western world – for benefit abuse?

'The council had successfully undertaken 29 prosecutions and applied 33 formal cautions and administrative penalties during 2003/04,' says the inspectors' report. Officially, then, there were 63 benefit abusers in Liverpool in 2003–4. This is a slander of

Boris Johnson proportions on Liverpudlians and their entrepreneurial vigour in making money out of the system.*

Ravenstone UK, a company specialising in covert surveillance, said, 'We investigated 400 of these cases [for the bus company Arriva]. Only 20 per cent we could prove were genuine. We found scores that were made up.'

Caught on film

Stephen Hayes, managing director of Quantum Enquiries and Surveillance, is part of the fightback on spurious compensation cases. His company covertly film people who are claiming incapacity. They say they can't walk six feet without sitting down; they get filmed tap-dancing round the Silverstone race track. Mr Hayes sent me his company's DVD.

The voiceover commentary quotes from the subject's depositions and it makes you smile at first, but there comes a point when you start to get quite irritable.

- The surveillance film showed a fellow playing rugby, running like a rabbit and making a heroic tackle. The voiceover says, 'The subject had a car accident. The whiplash and accompanying pain in his neck,

---

* Slip-and-trip claims in Liverpool's Knowsley rose from 350 a year in the 1990s to 1,500 in 2002 during the height of the Claims Direct and Accident Group commercial activity.

shoulders and both arms radiating to his lower back prevent even the simplest of tasks. He can walk backwards but he can't continue with his local authority duties or his leisure activities.'

- A woman is shown carrying a four-foot sack of fertiliser from a garden centre and opening the tailgate of her car to lift the sack in. 'Having slipped and fallen hard on a patch of oil in the office she cannot carry files and descend stairs. She can't reach above her head to the storage shelving. Walking is also difficult and a full day's work is now impossible.'

- A woman is shown carrying boxes of flowers to her car, loading them up and driving off. The voiceover says, 'Having fallen on an uneven footpath, this lady is now unable to properly manage her florist shop. She cannot drive. She cannot visit the market. She cannot lift even the lightest object. In addition, she is claiming for a member of staff to perform her own duties.'

- A workman is shown carrying a pallet and standing at a respectable height on scaffolding. 'This man doesn't deny he can perform some duties in the building trade, having fallen from scaffolding, injuring his arms and back. He is now nervous of heights and ladder climbing. He can never work on scaffolding or lift heavy objects. He is proud of the fact he has struggled back to work in a supervisory capacity only, ensuring he remains at ground level.'

- A man is shown driving around town and restocking the kiosk he owns on a mainline platform. 'This man was in a serious rail accident and was very fortunate he was not one of the fatalities. He admits he wants to work, but only locally at his home. He cannot now travel to the city. The memories of the accident have caused such mental scarring that he is now frightened of being transported in any form. Even a car. But especially by train. He cannot be near a train. He cannot look at a train. And the sound of one causes dizziness and sweating.'

- Before his accident, the subject was a post office driver of a seven-tonne truck transporting and lifting trolleys of mail. The accident was in his own car and in his own time. 'Now that he's unable to drive without discomfort, bend and walk without a limp, his employers have given him an admin position without such responsibilities.' The subject is seen driving and lifting and pushing trolleys.

- 'Falling down a flight of stairs at her job in a government department rendered the subject unable to work. She was practically confined to home and could not drive without immense pain. Couldn't bend [the subject is shown bending over a shopping trolley, balancing on one leg], walked with a pronounced limp and couldn't do anything one would normally regard as normal daily activities.' The subject is now shown filling up her car boot from the supermarket shop.

- A rubbish collector draws benefit for injuring his wrists but works freelance shifts for a competitor. A joiner fell off a ladder and 'couldn't put his hands above his head', but is shown working normally.

- A trench digger who'd had a trench collapse on him, trapping his lower body, gave evidence claiming that the levels of pain in performing simple tasks were '... indescribable. Any effort by the upper arms produces pain down the length of the body which requires long periods of rest.' He was shown working normally. A mother is shown lifting her baby joyfully above shoulder height: 'Lifting the child is impossible without assistance.'

Presumably, they present themselves in court in neck braces and walking frames; they flinch at loud noises and cower at the mildest question. People seem to be strangely reluctant to confront others with accusations of malingering, of exaggerating, of laying it on with a trowel. Sometimes, bafflingly so. For instance, in *Napier* v. *Chief Constable of Cambridgeshire Constabulary*, the judge had watched video footage of the claimant walking his dog and taking his child to and from school. Then he said, 'The claimant is [not] consciously exaggerating his symptoms when seen by doctors, or when he is sitting stiff-necked in court *as he has* [added emphasis], but the video evidence does lead me to the conclusion that the pain and stiffness he suffers in his neck is not as disabling as he has come to believe, and that when he is not thinking about it he can lead a fairly normal life.'

This is an annoyingly charitable interpretation of what is described. Perhaps the judge did not want to accuse the claimant of dishonesty or otherwise open up grounds for complaint or appeal. Such is the state we're in.

How disability compensation creates disability

It isn't new, this, any of it. One of the first effects of social insurance (apart from the splendid sense of security and comfort and support for the families of injured workers) was malingering. In his 1947 book, *German Experience with Social Insurance,* Walter Sulzbach said, 'Over a period of fifty years (1880–1930) and despite major advancements in medical science and doctor access, it took the average patient under the compulsory health insurance scheme a longer time to recover. In 1885, a year after socialised health insurance began, the average number of sick days each year was 14.1. In 1900, the average had gone up to 17.6; in 1925 it had increased to 24.4 days; and by 1930, it was 29.9 days.'

The effects are not straightforward. Whatever the psychological mechanisms at work, paying people to be incapable seems to make them less capable.

George Mendelson's paper 'Outcome-related Compensation' quotes from the Sanders and Meyers study of 1986. This compared the period of work disability of two groups of US railwaymen. Both groups had suffered back injuries – one group had been injured at work and the other group had been injured off duty. The two groups were matched for type of injury and gender. The 35 victims on compensation were off for an average of 14.2 months, and the 30 subjects injured off duty were away 4.9 months. The 'financial rewards of compensation', concluded the authors, were responsible for the difference.

According to a 1997 paper on the effect of compensation on how people report pain and disability, 'Patients seeking or receiving compensation for chronic low back pain reported more pain, depression and disability than a matched group without compensation involvement.'

A study published in the *New England Journal of Medicine* on crash injuries before and after Saskatchewan's introduction of no-fault insurance found that 'the elimination of compensation for pain and suffering is associated with a decreased incidence and improved prognosis of whiplash injury'.

When there was no financial advantage to claiming whiplash, the claims fell off. And, even more important, a faster resolution of claims seems to be linked with faster recovery, less intense pain and fewer depressive symptoms, according to J. David Cassidy and his fellow authors.

The International Underwriters Association estimated in a study in March 2003 that the chance of a paraplegic's returning to employment is 50 per cent in Scandinavia; 32 per cent in the USA; but only 14 per cent in the UK.

But scepticism puts the medical professional in an impossible position, as Dr Michael Sharpe shows with this ordinary case example.

'A 25-year-old man presented for admission at a psychiatric hospital saying he was frightened of what he was seeing'. 'He reported distressing experiences including seeing his friend's head rotate 360 degrees "like in *The Exorcist*". He had a history of poly-drug misuse and was due to appear in court on a drug-related charge. He appeared to be genuinely distressed and did not have evidence of drug intoxication. His symptoms resolved over several days. It remained unclear whether the psychosis was real, malingered or "hysterical" although the presence of apparently genuine distress was thought to favour the latter.'

Of course, whiplash exists. Backs go wrong. Some people can't get out of bed because their backs are so bad. But it's the easiest sort of lie to pull off because there is no Geiger counter that detects pain. All we have to go on is what the patient tells the doctor. We all have different pain thresholds, we all have different tolerances, and we all have different incentives to ignore or embrace the pain. And we all have a different sense of the truth. It is, as we know, perfectly possible to damage oneself enough, to disable oneself enough to become eligible for compensation.

And it works the other way round. One woman loses a leg and is permanently disabled. Another loses hers (as she did in the 7/7 bomb) and the following year she runs a marathon.

How does a doctor go about disbelieving the patient – especially when the consequences can be fatal? ('I told them! I warned them! I'm not to be trusted! That's why I was forced to do untrustworthy things!') Hysterical disorders are still disorders. Self-inflicted wounds are still wounds. Whether (and how, and in what sum) they deserve compensation – that's a very different, and very difficult, question.

Malingering and Illness Deception is a collection of papers edited and introduced by Peter Halligan, Chris Bass and David Oakley. They are psychologists who – daringly, considering the vested interests ranged against them – examine psychological disabilities in a critical manner.

Obviously, they don't say all medical claims are bogus. But they do – disruptively – suggest that the level of faking, or fraud, or malingering, or conscious and unconscious deception is much higher than the conventional pieties allow.

Their paper says, '... people who engage in illness deception are not ill, nor are they mad – they simply lack the moral faculties that we assume most in society take for granted.' And they go on to say that conflating medical disorder with social deviance – 'by uncritically endorsing the medicalisation of social deviance – serves neither medicine nor society and ends up denying one of the most fundamental characteristics of human nature'.

Why has incapacity tripled while health inexorably improves? they ask. The answer, in all its academic complexity, is worth getting to grips with:

'At the end of the twentieth century, a cultural shift within medicine occurred which resulted in the acceptance of a growing number of symptom-based illnesses and a more tolerant attitude to illness deception. By blurring this distinction between wilful deception and medical disorder, illness behaviours could be explained in terms of an ever-expanding list of psychopathologies.'

I'm lying, and that's the truth

'Even persistent lying about illness has now been defined as an illness,' says Theodore Dalrymple.

And, for those inclined to scoff at Dr Dalrymple, here's a short passage from www.impaccusa.com, a website selling compensation solutions: 'Some Cumulative Trauma Disorder sufferers may exaggerate their disability to assure others that they really do have a problem. This is called "symptom magnification" and is not faking. It is a common complication of the CTD problem.'

∿

In these matters, logic is very often a false friend. You can reason yourself into anything. And there is more than enough in the culture, if you select carefully, to persuade yourself that early retirement on full pay is not just legitimate but richly deserved.

The police officer has a job he's sick of. He's always done his duty. He's paid taxes all his life, he's always given more than he's taken, he's undergone stress that an office worker couldn't conceive of, he's been in physical danger trying to keep the lid on society and always hampered by rules, regulations and paperwork as if he were a clerk. He has never, ever taken a bribe whatsoever in his life. Practically never. Not what you'd call a bribe. But the abuse he's taken! From ethnics. From drunken, bingeing women. From kids. From his own kids! And his back is – as his father said, or possibly his grandfather – giving him 'gyp'. Walking's difficult sometimes, a shooting pain all down his leg. He's been in the service 27 years and is eligible for early retirement on medical grounds. He's never taken his full quota of sick days. Not like others who've taken months off work with hangovers through the years. And everyone – practically everyone – everyone who wants to – takes early retirement if they've got a bad back. It's a perk of the coppering job. Like free newspapers for journalists. It's traditional. It's expected. Actually, you're disloyal for not doing it. You're spoiling it for the others. One bad apple can infect the whole barrel.

Being an honest sort of person, he doesn't like to lie, so assembles the evidence that his back is worse than it is, especially on examination day. He adjusts the average pain to the levels of the worst days. He may be having a good day on the appointment day, but he doesn't want to give the doctor the wrong impression, so he hobbles in slowly. He sits painfully. He struggles into a prone position and finds he can't lift his leg. That is, he probably could if there was a fire, but he has to give the doctor an accurate impression of what his condition is, even though it isn't very easy just at the moment. But he doesn't want to mislead the medical profession with this temporary rally in his condition.

If he says he's feeling better suddenly he will lose very substantial cash benefits. You need them at that end of life. It might be worth £100,000. That's a very nice cushion in life; with a little income from here and there, doing odd jobs on a cash basis he'll be well set up for a decent retirement – which, incidentally, he has paid for from his taxes.

So that pain is very important to keep in the forefront of the mind.

And that is how police officers can explain their early retirement to themselves.

However, try this thought experiment. Imagine the incentives were the other way round. In some parallel world, the policeman has to pay £100,000 if he doesn't complete his full term of service. You can be sure that the only people taking early retirement would be so disabled they couldn't get out of bed. This isn't to say that is desirable, just that human behaviour adjusts to the incentives that are on offer.

It's Stressing
Me Out

'Workers with stressful jobs are more than twice as likely to die from heart disease.'

Trades Union Congress

This statement isn't in any way exceptional in the language of today. It fits with every part of our culture. And yet it may not mean anything at all. It's as useful as a horoscope. ('You are creative and have a good sense of humour but you are often not appreciated at work as much as you should be.')

Because – ask yourself – what's a 'worker'? What's a 'stressful job'? What does 'twice as likely' mean? And what do they mean by 'heart disease'? Every part of the statement is tendentious and politicised, and has an ulterior purpose. It would need someone of Tony Blair's skill with words to twist and torture this sentence to make it give up the desired meaning.

In fact, we need no medical knowledge to say the assertion is drivel. Airline pilots are not twice as likely to die of heart disease as Parliamentary sketch writers. And Parliamentary sketch writers are not twice as likely to die of stress as Parliamentarians. You would have to be a revenue-producing part of the 'stress-busting' industry to accept the idea at face value.

Jobs aren't stressful in themselves. Teaching self-righteous, overweight, violent, foul-mouthed, drug-dealing 13-year-olds without being able to whack them when they tell you to fuck off for being a useless loser or they'll rape you after school – that might be considered stressful. But there are heroic individuals who embrace that vocation and some do it with ease and come out stronger. At the other end of the spectrum, washing up in Fenwick's restaurant (my first job) was so stressful for me that I quit after six hours – no one showed me how to load the dishwasher properly.

Whatever 'stress' is (and current definitions are very loose) it has to do with the individual's reaction to a job, how a person copes with a job than with the job itself. Angela Patmore, a stress heretic, says, '"Exhaustion due to overwork", "depression" and "anxiety" are feasible explanations for a patient being unable to work. But "stress" is not.'

The concept of stress at work as an illness, a disease, is an important part of the compensation culture. If you can prove your boss has made you ill – with asbestosis, for instance – you can claim compensation for your slow and painful degeneration. But this concept has led step by step to an entirely new regime. Now you can diagnose yourself as sick with stress; this diagnosis will be accepted by your doctor (that's his job); and you can claim compensation in the form of civil damages or sickness benefit or early retirement if you work for the government.

~~

'Working for unreasonable and unfair bosses leads to dangerously high blood pressure.'

Trades Union Congress

This is another facile generalisation. Or, as we used to say, rubbish. Because life isn't fair, as we tell our children, the task for us all is to develop strategies for dealing with unreasonable and unfair bosses. If we can't cope with the unreasonable and the unfair, we will go mad. Unreasonable bosses are everywhere. Their job is to get us to do slightly more than we want to.

The only reason I don't develop dangerously high blood pressure from reading statements such as the one above is that I have created a Zen strategy for calming myself when confronted with apparently neutral statements that conceal a raging political purpose. I go to my happy place.

'Workers exposed to stress for at least half their working lives are 25 per cent more likely to die from a heart attack and have 50 per cent higher odds of suffering a fatal stroke.'

Trades Union Congress

It's harder and harder to get to your happy place, the more of this you absorb. Because, if the number of people suffering from stress has doubled (see below), what's happening to deaths from heart disease? Rocketing? Soaring? Increasingly slightly? Is there actually an epidemic of workers keeling over scrabbling at their chests? The death rate from heart disease and stroke among the under-75s has fallen 27 per cent since 1996, and is set to reduce further. Admittedly, that figure comes from the Department of Health but it could still be halfway true.

According to *Worked to Death*, a collection of articles from the Health and Safety Executive's journal *Hazards*, 'the number of people saying they suffer from stress and stress-related conditions caused or made worse by work has more than doubled since 1990, according to latest HSE [Health and Safety Executive] figures (*Hazards* 81). The "estimated" prevalence of stress and stress-related conditions rose from 829 cases per 100,000 workers in 1990, to 1,700 per 100,000 in 2001/02. HSE figures show that last year 13.4 million lost working days were attributed to stress, anxiety or depression, with an estimated 265,000 new cases of stress.'

These figures are all based on surveys of people who self-assess their condition. 'Are you stressed at work? Is your work stressful?'

Angela Patmore says sardonically, 'American employees apparently think they work longer hours than medieval peasants', and that 'the average American now works a full nine weeks longer than the average Western European worker'. Which may be why they are very much richer than we are.

Patmore suggests that helplessness and hopelessness may be the real killers. This is the exact opposite of 'stress'.

You Can't Blame Me!

'Am I my brother's keeper?'

Genesis

The closest to indignation I ever saw the cool English journalist Alexander Chancellor was when he was talking about a dinner for four in upstate New York in the 1980s. The establishment refused to bring a second bottle of wine to his table. Had the diners had a second glass each and then had an accident, the restaurant could have been sued. We gasped and rolled our eyes at the story. Those Yanks. Only in America!

It could never happen here – or could it? It's on the way. Police officers can be held responsible if anyone dies within 24 hours of leaving police custody. Thus, Surrey police spent £9,000 in 2005 giving drunks free taxi rides home. Superintendent Martin Parker said: 'If we did not provide a method for a released person to get home and they were killed while making their own way,

84

a death-in-custody investigation into Surrey police would be started and would cost millions.'

It's here, it's there, it's everywhere.

An Australian tried to sue Geelong Football Club for allowing him to get too drunk at a lunch in 2003. 'In Supreme Court documents seen by the *Geelong Advertiser*, Gregory Allan Clifford claims he consumed "excessive quantities of liquor" supplied by the club at a president's lunch about two years ago.

'Mr Clifford claims he fell down a set of stairs at the club function and severely injured himself. In the civil lawsuit against the club he claims the club should have exercised reasonable care to conduct the function in a way where people drinking were reasonably safe.'

It's not obvious what steps the club might have taken (people can drink very large amounts at sporting lunches). A personal security guard behind each drinker's chair? Like nannies behind the chairs of five-year-olds at the Duke of Westminster's kiddy parties? But wouldn't that stigmatise the drinkers as incapable? Couldn't they then sue for injury to feelings and loss of reputation? Surely the safest thing would be not to serve alcohol at all.

↝

It might have come to that in Australia, unless a court in New South Wales had ruled against this 'social host' principle in February 2005 – at least, insofar as it applies to drinking. Some adults had tried to reignite the barbecue in the early hours of the morning, not by breathing on it – which probably would have worked – but by throwing a bottle of methylated spirit into it. In the resulting fire, a woman got burned and sued the property owners, who'd gone to bed leaving the partygoers (all of whom were over 18) unsupervised. Justice Tobias rejected the claim, saying that to allow it would eliminate alcohol from Australian social life.

In Russia, a French electrician died from too much vodka. It was ruled that he was the victim of a 'workplace accident' even though he wasn't at work, or even working at the time. He died of alcohol poisoning after a night of Russian drinking with indigenous colleagues in Nalchik, southern Russia.

The widow's social security fund refused to consider this to be an industrial accident or to pay her the pension she would have received if her husband had died in harness. But the courts concluded that the man's death was indeed an industrial accident because work duties had required him to attend the party. His employers should therefore share the blame for his demise.

Wheels of misfortune

An Ontario woman who got drunk at an office party and crashed her car sued her employer for allowing her to drive. The company had offered her a cab ride or a night's accommodation if she gave up her keys, but it did them no good in court. Linda Hunt won more than $300,000 from her employers after arguing that she should have been stopped from driving home in a snowstorm after a 1994 Christmas party.

The judge assessed the lady's damages from the resulting accident at $1.2 million, but reduced that by three-quarters to reflect her own fault in the matter. She was mostly to blame for insisting on drunkenly driving into a car crash but she got $300,000 because the judge declared that the employers were 25 per cent to blame as they had failed to monitor her alcohol consumption.

In 2002, a drunken woman from Winnipeg, Kim Simon, was found outside her home with her pants pulled down, her jacket open and a cut lip. Does that bring back memories for you, too?

She nearly froze to death so she set about suing the city, emergency personnel and the taxi driver who dropped her off at home. Emergency workers had dropped Ms Simon off at her residence but things must have gone wrong somehow (we don't exactly know how except that it obviously wasn't her fault). The emergency personnel and the taxi driver were to blame: they should have made sure she was safely inside her house before leaving.

That sort of drunken reasoning will be familiar to some of us degenerates: 'I'm lonely, I'm angry, I'm unhappy, and if I am, why isn't everyone? *And* I'm bleeding! My pants are undone! I'll get so unhappy they'll really be sorry! I want money!'

You can bet on it

According to a *Guardian* story, 'A ruined French gambler yesterday [14 November 2005] sued a casino for failing to prevent him losing his money. Jean-Philippe Bryk, 44, claimed the Grand Café casino in the spa town of Vichy owed him a duty of "information, advice and loyalty".

'Mr Bryk won some £11,000 on his first two visits in 1995, but lost nearly £500,000 over the next eight years. "The staff watched him get addicted, watched him lose control, and kept inviting him back with free dinners," said his lawyer, Gilles-Jean Portejoie.'

After a night of drinking, Dustin W. Bailey walked out of a Teays Valley bar in West Virginia, crossed the street and ended up having a rest underneath an idling tractor-trailer delivering supplies to a pizza restaurant. The truck killed him when the driver pulled forward.

Nearly two years after the accident, Bailey's mother started suing everyone – the pizza restaurant, the truck's driver, the truck's owner and the bar's owner – because, she says, they all failed to take steps to keep her son alive.

Chief Deputy John Dailey of the sheriff's department has a different view of the liability: 'If anyone should be blamed for that death, it's that guy who climbed under the truck.'

I blame the mother. She should be suing herself. And her mother too (these things never start where they seem to start).

'I'm suing you for failing to realise how stupid I am...'

Public Safety is the Number One Priority

In 1994, the term 'at risk' featured 2,000 times in UK newspapers. In 2003 that figure had risen to over 25,000. Health and safety has been a growth industry like no other.

We love a scare. We whoop them up. We celebrate fear. The carcinogenic pill, mobile-phone masts' electromagnetic fields and radiation, genetically modified foods, the end of the world, MMR jabs, BSE, *E. coli*, salmonella, Sudan B, SARS, microwaves, domestic appliances, avian flu, stress, coffee, sun rays, global warming, global cooling, global terrorism, second-hand smoke, too-fat men, too-thin women, children drowning in swimming pools, paedophiles filming the nativity play – there is a willing market out there for any passing alarm.

Had the whole health-and-safety concept been a top-down operation like the Inland Revenue, many of us would collaborate to frustrate it as far as we could. But a crucial compensation mechanism (which produced a compensation culture) has given the health-and-safety industry enormous reach and power. Compensation put punitive power in the hands of individuals and rewarded them for slights, grievances, snubs, psychological damage and overwork (now called stress). Health-and-safety protocols have access to the private life of everyone in the country, and all our personal relationships and many social arrangements fall into its ambit.

Andrew Dismore MP (a personal-injury lawyer and prominent 'compensation-culture denier') talked out the Brazier Bill in Parliament, which was intended to ease the liability of adult volunteers. But even he says this: 'The health-and safety culture has got completely out of hand.' It's true. Dismore's judgment was supported, probably by accident, by Jonathan Rees, the deputy chief executive of the Health and Safety Executive. He told the Constitutional Affairs inquiry into the compensation question that the risk-assessment process was not designed to increase risk aversion. He referred to the report of the professor who had to fill in a 69-page risk assessment before he went on a field visit. 'That is ridiculous,' Mr Rees said, 'and we have said it is ridiculous, but there is no doubt that that exists.'

He asked why it existed. He wasn't able to say why.

Also, the St John Ambulance says this: '... if one of these first-aiders witnesses an accident in the street, they are, these days, faced with a dilemma: do they just walk on by, or do they provide first aid? In general, the first course of action exposes them to no risk. However, the second course presents substantial risk, i.e. that if due to their intervention the outcome for the "victim" is adversely affected, then they are likely to be sued. There are many incidents of this kind, e.g. the injured motorcyclist whose crash helmet is removed, perhaps to provide resuscitation, but who as a result suffers damage to his neck.'

To return to Andrew Dismore. He went on to say, 'That is nothing to do with being sued: it is connected with the self-perpetuating health-and-safety profession, which can make a living only out of frightening people.'

However, it is *precisely* 'to do with being sued'.

Sunny side up – not!

St George's Day in Bromham, near Chippenham, 2006. Three hundred villagers were on the point of launching their fundraising British breakfast in the community centre. But the charity event was cancelled because of a health-and-safety warning against frying eggs. The local council's guidelines state that volunteers should not prepare 'protein-based foods' without proper training.

Peter Wallis, chairman of the local school's Parent–Teacher Association, said, 'I was astonished to discover that we had to adhere to health-and-safety regulations to cook people breakfast. We have to provide evidence that whoever is handling the food has been trained to do so. We spoke to other schools in the area and decided that because people were not properly qualified in food preparation we had to cancel the event. This is just plain daft.

'These breakfasts have been going on for many years and we've never poisoned anyone. We are looking at sending some of our parents on training courses, but with the turnover of members each year that could be too expensive.'

The local MP, Philip Davies, added, 'The regulations also say the eggs have to be chilled literally from when we buy them to when they are cooked to be eaten. What we have done for years and years is to buy them and take them home overnight to someone's home but that is not allowed any more. Keeping them at some parent's house overnight is not sufficient evidence they have been stored properly.'

Councillor Mark Baker, vice chairman of education on Tory-held Wiltshire County Council, said the authority's health and safety guidelines were not legally binding.

But legally binding or not, the guidelines are affirmative – especially should it come to a lawsuit with some parent suing for an upset stomach. Is it worth the risk of losing your house because someone says your egg made them ill? Or is safer just to cancel the event?

'In order to cover against someone contracting a stomach ailment and then deciding to sue, it would have cost the football club more than £250 for one afternoon to run the barbecue. Goodbye also to the local annual tradition of 'pole-walking' on a greased telegraph pole in a seaside Welsh village, deemed uninsurable though no one had actually hurt themselves seriously doing it. No one dares go ahead without cover. It is happening everywhere: fêtes and fund-raising events shredded of anything that might carry potential for injury, and thus potential for fun.' (Jim White, *Daily Telegraph*)

In 2005, a property management firm responsible for three Lancashire jobcentres advised the Department for Work and Pensions that ceiling and wall decorations posed a health-and-safety risk. A small Christmas tree was fine as long as new lights (either with a 12-month warranty or tested in the past year) were used. In a separate festival ban, it was reported that the management of a jobcentre in Peterborough had prohibited decorations entirely. The fear was that staff might hurt themselves while putting up holly or that tinsel would add to the fire hazard created by the extra paper, plastic and pine.

The appropriate minister, the Prime Minister, the Health and Safety Commission, the Health and Safety

Executive will all say, if asked, that there is absolutely no need to take these absurd precautions. But the precautions are nonetheless taken. The activity appeals to the very deepest instincts of officials: all those keen, off-duty policemen who prosecute motorists because their number plate numerals are a quarter-inch too far apart; or playground attendants who prevent a child going into a playground because she's half an inch too tall; or the train timetable that has numbers a tenth of an inch too small for the disability regulations.

Long time aglow . . .

Organisers of a traditional night-time Christmas procession had to replace flaming torches with glow sticks.

The procession, in Looe, Cornwall, has attracted about 500 people and has taken place for 20 years without injury. However, officials from the harbour authority and the council said the risk of fire was too great with torches. The mayor pointed out that there would be people with long hair present.

The council spent £350 on buying 500 glow sticks. 'It's an absolute joke,' said a local, John Andrews. 'How can you have a torchlight procession with glow sticks? We'll be the laughing stock of the county.'

~

According to *The Times* of 28 January 2005, a hamlet in Wales was denied doorstep delivery by the Royal Mail because of the health-and-safety dangers to a postman inherent in climbing over a stile.

Conked out

Norwich City Council attracted much mockery in 2001 with its plans to fell 17 mature horse chestnut trees in order to stop children hurting themselves. Children were throwing sticks at the branches. Conkers falling into the road were deemed a danger to passing motorists. Also, the resultant mulch was designated a slip hazard for pedestrians.

In 2005, Havering Council in east London cut down dozens of healthy trees saying they could be sued if people slipped on fallen fruit. The head of street care, Zulfiqar Ali, said the council had never been sued by anyone over rotten, slippery fruit on the pavement but the potential existed for such action.

A hundred four-foot-high yew trees near a children's playground on a council estate were uprooted by Bristol Council in March 2006 for fear that children might eat the leaves or berries and be poisoned (not that the berries are poisonous).

Parents had complained. The council performed a risk assessment. The 'safest option', they said, was to uproot them all.

Yew tree leaves are extremely unpleasant to eat (it's an evolutionary defence against yew-leaf-eating children). You also have to consume a lot – 'several handfuls' according to naturalist Trevor Beer – before suffering toxic effects. Nonetheless, the safest option, to avoid being sued by parents claiming their children had been poisoned, was deracination and the incinerator.

Yew trees near playgrounds are one thing. But what about yew trees in graveyards? Why are children allowed in graveyards at all, with their deadly gravestones (see below) and poisonous trees?

We may be slightly ahead of America in this regard, though the problem certainly exists over there: 'Swings and other fun elements are disappearing fast from southern Florida playgrounds under lawyering pressure'. 'To say no running on the playground seems crazy,' says Broward County School Board member Robin Bartleman, whose six-year-old daughter is disappointed in the playground at Everglades Elementary in Weston. 'But your feelings change when you're in a closed-door meeting with lawyers.'

The UK's Commission for Architecture and the Built Environment in 2004 reported the removal of a swing from a playing field because it faced the sun and could blind children. Another regular occurrence, it said, was the removal of three-in-a-row swings because the outer swings could hit the one in the middle.

There is no legal need to remove swings. But Ryan Simonds, a five-year-old boy at the time, fell off a swing and broke his arm, and his mother sued for compensation. She won £4,250. The judge said the school was negligent and that the swings should have been immobilised or taped off out of playtime. But the case was appealed and the High Court said in 2003: 'Oh, for God's sake! Don't be so bloody stupid!' (I paraphrase.)

Mr Justice Gross said that if 'word got out' that the boy had won his case 'the probability is sports days and other pleasurable sporting events will simply not take place ... Such events could easily become uninsurable, or at prohibitive cost.'

A grave situation

A six-year-old boy was killed in Harrogate in July 2000 when a gravestone fell on him. There was no administrative reaction until the parents were given £33,000 in compensation in September 2003. The sum was in recognition of the trauma suffered by Reuben's mother, Jeanette Powell, who saw her son's injuries when the memorial stone was lifted off him.

When the award was made, councils across Britain snapped into graveyard action. They inspected millions of gravestones and laid flat tens of thousands (and possibly hundreds of thousands) of stones that were deemed to pose a risk.

'The safety of the public is absolutely paramount, including those relatives that are visiting the graves,' Gerald Royston of Melton Mowbray Council said.

It's one of those things people say. If the safety of the public were absolutely paramount the gravestones would never have been allowed up and we'd be kept out of streets where there's traffic, and certainly wouldn't be allowed into kitchens, with all the pointed utensils lying around.

What the councillor actually means is that 'the safety of the public purse is absolutely paramount'. Reuben had been killed three years before the award was made, during which time few, if any, gravestones were laid flat. It was the compensation that triggered the activity.

Health and safety figures indicate there have been 13 nasty gravestone accidents, including half a dozen fatalities, since 1982.

Edinburgh council observed, 'So far we have inspected almost 13,000 memorials and have had to lay over 3,000 flat ... We are very lucky that no one has been killed or seriously injured in Edinburgh by a gravestone that has fallen on them.'

It's an odd use of the phrase 'very lucky'. What with a national total of 13 nasty accidents in 25 years with – let's guess – a billion visits through cemeteries, the odds are that Edinburgh would have been astronomically unlucky to have suffered a gravestone accident.

Nor is the action all one-way. Flat gravestones are themselves a risk. They are a danger. They constitute a trip hazard. Councils may consider themselves 'very lucky' that no one has fallen over a lowered stone and hurt their head on another firmly set, solid-as-the-Bank-of-England gravestone that is standing strong and proud because it has been reinforced by safety-conscious council workers.

We can add this to the calculation: in Stoke-on-Trent, nearly £20,000 in compensation has been paid out to people because the council failed to give notice of laying the gravestones down.

Some of us may feel the level of risk is functionally insignificant. But the train of events that the risk has caused is by no means insignificant or frivolous. All local authorities are involved, along with several big insurance companies, and industry associations such as the Institute of Cremation and Cemetery Management and the Association of Burial Authorities are all actively involved, too.

Employers worry that workers in cemeteries will be prosecuted if someone is injured by a memorial that they have identified as unstable: they recommend immediate laying flat to avoid any such risk. Sam Weller of the Association of Burial Authorities thinks it's all got out of proportion. He points out that the risk of prosecutions is very slight, but the risk of causing needless distress to the bereaved is absolutely certain. He recommends alternatives to laying down memorials.

'Modern memorials have been described as accidents waiting to happen,' says Mr Weller. 'Their basic design renders them unstable and risk assessments are finding up to 80 per cent dangerous among those installed in recent years. This is clearly not acceptable.

'However, the National Audit Office has reported that hospitals could be killing up to 34,000 patients a year because of mistakes made by staff. Falling memorials in cemeteries have caused three deaths in the past six years. This is not something that calls for the draconian action that some authorities have instigated.'

It might also be noted that, although 80 per cent of these headstones are unstable, they cause almost no injuries. If no compensation culture existed, we would simply take more care of our children in graveyards.

A British primary school cancelled its traditional Shrove Tuesday pancake race when its insurance premiums quadrupled and the company demanded 25 marshals line a 50-yard race route. Publicity about the plight caused another insurer to step in with a more reasonable premium, so long as the school limit the number of entrants and spectators. 'A spokesman for the British Insurance Brokers' Association said the UK was an increasingly litigious society, and people wanted to cover their backs should an accident occur.'

'At 11 o'clock last night, I received a phone call from the secretary of one of the people involved in the campaign, who told me that her son's secondary school in Exeter had abandoned its sports day last week because it had rained the previous night and the school was worried about being sued.'

Julian Brazier, in the 2004 debate on his
Volunteering Bill in the Commons

~

Meals-on-wheels officials in Gloucestershire were preparing to distribute paper napkins to elderly people. The napkins had tips printed on them telling the old people how to avoid being a crime victim. The initiative was suspended abruptly when someone realised no safety assessment had been made of the choking hazard, should pensioners put the napkins into their mouths. The initiative eventually went ahead, but critics said the episode encouraged the portrayal of aged persons as senile.

~

In 2005, a supermarket's plan to sell Christmas puddings with 'lucky sixpences' was prevented by a health and safety ruling. Sainsbury's, which spent months looking for the out-of-circulation coins, says it is not allowed to insert them into the puddings because they 'constitute a choking hazard'.

The Health and Safety Executive has decided that carrying paint on a bus is a hazard to the public and it is prohibited unless the tin of paint is carried in two containers – a sealed pot and a bag – and is not left unattended on a parcel shelf, where it could slide and tip, burst open and spread across the floor. A pensioner, Brian Heale, was thrown off a Cardiff bus for carrying his hazardous can. And rightly so. If there had been an accident (had he stumbled and dropped the unbagged can on someone's knee), the bus company would have been liable for a compensation claim.

Of ladders and doors

Moscow State Circus was warned in July 2003 that an acrobat performing above stepladder height would have to wear a hard hat or risk losing its insurance cover.

Police called in to investigate a broken stained-glass window at a church in Rochdale refused to inspect the damage because they did not have specialist 'ladder training'.

After a woman caught her foot in the new doors at BBC Birmingham, the corporation issued a memo, 'Revolving Security Door User Instructions', advising staff on how to use a revolving door. To do any less would be to open the management to a charge of negligence and indifference to the safety of their staff.

In 2005, 19 schools across Renfrewshire in Scotland banned pupils from taking part in after-school soccer over fears of getting sued. They were banned because volunteer coaches were not covered by the schools' insurance schemes for after-class games.

But the most surprising element of the story was this: council leaders had told head teachers that if children were injured – including injuries in vehicle accidents on the way to games – the organisers would be held responsible.

This kind of information is cultural rather than legal. Any claim based on such a proposition would surely be thrown out of court. 'I was taking my son to practice and drove my car into a tree. He is paralysed and you owe me £3 million.' Since certain key verdicts in the last two or three years (see pages 202–209), this sort of claim fails. But authorities are still acting on the assumption of compensation. The culture prevails.

And there's another significant question: why should a child injured playing sport be entitled to compensation by the school? If parents are worried by the cost of caring for a disabled child, why don't they take out their own insurance?

The Borough of Barnet was found liable for multimillion-pound damages after a pupil contracted

E. coli on a school trip to a farm (suffering brain damage and paralysis). Terrible thing, of course, but there are many people who would argue that it's not reasonable for a school to be liable for a disease one of their pupils catches while visiting a farm.

Dowling v. *London Borough of Barnet and Bowman's Farm,*
January 2000

∿

A survey of 100 obstetricians suggests that half of all caesarean births (that is, 55,000 a year) carried out aren't medically necessary and this costs the NHS more than £80 million a year, says 'Caesarean Births in Britain', a report written by obstetricians and sociologists. The number of caesareans has doubled in eight years. The authors suggest that a fear of litigation is at the root of the increase.

Professor Colin Francombe of Middlesex Hospital is a
co-author of the survey

∿

Be Safe is the Department of Education's booklet on work experience. It is a model of its kind. Nothing could be better calculated to induce sceptical contempt among our reckless youth (especially the children they most want to reach). This new doctrine of washing your hands *before* using the toilet as well as after – that's really going to catch on.

Here is some of their advice:

- Never play practical jokes – they can KILL!
- Wash your hands, using soap and water or suitable cleanser, before you eat a meal and before and after using the toilet
- Close drawers.
- Both male and female animals can cause death or injury. You can avoid accidents by not entering areas containing animals unless it is necessary.
- Always wash your hands after contact with animals.
- TRY THIS CROSSWORD: 3 Across: You must do this before and after you stop work for a meal or go to the toilet. 4, 4, 5.
- Falls, sometimes from quite low levels, can cause death or serious injuries – FACT.
- Animals can pass on serious or fatal diseases to humans – FACT.
- One moment without the protection of Personal Protective Equipment could result in serious injury – FACT.
- Compressed air can kill – don't play with it – FACT.

Learning from experience?

'A few weeks ago, I received a letter from a C of E school in south London. "Dear Mary," it said. "Thank you for supporting our work experience programme. Lucy will have been fully briefed in her Personal and Social

Education lessons about work experience. With regard to Health and safety (sic), it is vital that all students are briefed about this on the first morning of the placement. Signed: Miss I. Smith (Assistant Work Experience Co-ordinator)."

'For a second, I bridled at the bossiness. I picked up the phone to call Miss Smith to deliver a high-minded little whinge about the importance of being polite to those offering pupils places, but I stopped before dialling.

'The letter was probably sent as a matter of course, just to show parents that the school cared. It was pathetic of me to complain.

'Soon after the letter arrived, so did Lucy, a quiet 15-year-old carrying a transparent, mauve-tinted folder. Out of the folder came a sheet of paper called "Checklist For Employer's Briefing to Students", which she handed to me, shyly. Miss Smith, it seemed, was serious.

'So we took our coffee out into *The Spectator*'s garden and tackled the first instruction. "Explain who will be in immediate charge of the student in the workplace and ensure that line managers are aware of their responsibilities under health and safety legislation," said the checklist. "I am your line manager, and I am aware," I said to Lucy.

'"Next, explain the safety policy and emphasise the student's personal responsibilities. Distribute and explain relevant safety literature and introduce students to key safety people. Describe any areas which students must not visit for safety reasons," said the list. "Let's skip straight on to 'Workplace Hazards'," I said firmly.

'"Explain the importance of keeping drawers and cupboard doors shut and the safe positioning of loose telephones," said the list. "Tell students where lavatories are and explain the use of barrier creams." What is the use of barrier creams? I asked Lucy. She looked at the floor.

'The list continued: "Check that students understand the importance of following health and safety rules and the possible consequence of disobeying them." Did many of your friends go to meat-packing factories for their work experience? I asked Lucy. "No," she said, "mostly media."

'On day two, we started early, hoping to get through "Emergency Procedures" before sundown. "Explain that all accidents must be reported, that all injuries, no matter how small, must be entered in the accident book, and where the accident book is kept."

'To my great surprise, I found *The Spectator* accident book under a volume of Sir Woodrow Wyatt's poems. It is a nice-looking blue hardback notebook with a red spine, containing a single entry on the first page: "8/2/1985. Henrietta Sykes: splinter in thumb under nail" '.

Mary Wakefield, *The Spectator*

In deep water – or not

Lord Phillips told the Commons All-Party Constitutional Affairs Select Committee about a visit to his old school, Bryanston: 'I am chairman of the governors of my old school, and when in the past I went down there, I would have a swim before breakfast with a member of staff. I'm now told by the bursar that we can't swim unless there is a lifeguard present. When I ask why not, I am told it is because the insurers require it.'

The school insurers require it because the lack of a lifeguard constitutes negligence, and health and safety protocols will be produced as evidence in the resulting claim for compensation.

Is it reasonable? It's true that swimming without a lifeguard will inevitably result in a certain number of deaths a year. The presence of a lifeguard will inevitably save a certain number of lives a year. The annual number of recreational-swimming deaths out there in unsupervised rivers and waterways is in the low twenties. Is it worth it? What are the odds of a boy's drowning in an unsupervised pool at Bryanston? I know how many boys drowned in the swimming pools of my two schools in the 1960s: *none*.

In April 2006, a lifeguard instructor and her health and safety officer husband were prevented from taking their three children into the toddlers' pool at Sedgemoor Splash in Bridgwater, Somerset.

The parents were told that their children needed individual supervision. Three children require three adults. Mrs Keren Townsend (a former swimming pool manager herself) said, 'It was absolutely ridiculous. The children are all happy and confident in the water and we can hold on to all three of them. This attitude is going to cause more drownings because swimming is such a vital skill.

'Councils should be encouraging more parents to put their kids into the water so that children can learn in a safe environment. If children don't go with their mum and dad when they're young, then they try swimming alone or with their friends in rivers or quarries. It's a recipe for disaster.'

The council said, 'The child admission policy is designed to protect the safety of all visitors. This policy is based on guidance offered by the Institute of Sport and Recreation Management and is recognised as an approved code of practice.'

The fact is, had the Townsends had an accident in the pool, of course, they would have been advised by claims farmers that they could sue the pool managers for allowing them to endanger their children.

Not fair

Health and safety officers have closed Britain's last 'moving staircase' fairground attraction, even though the ride has operated in complete safety since it opened in 1933. The owner of the camp at Felixstowe says he believes the Cakewalk is the last one left in Britain: 'Inspectors from the Health and Safety Executive have ruled that it must be closed because it no longer meets modern safety standards.'

In 2005, the firing of a salute on Remembrance Sunday in Walton, Essex, was cancelled on health-and-safety grounds. The decision was taken 'to protect onlookers from debris that might be blown back to shore by the wind'.

War veterans, who had survived larger dangers than this, expressed surprise.

When helpers couldn't help

In 2004, three women in Henley bled to death as the police watched from a distance, refusing to allow them to be helped by the paramedics (who were present as well). The case bewildered everyone who read about it, but it's all consistent and explicable, and mandated by health and safety.

An estranged husband with a gun jumped over a garden fence during a barbecue, pursued his ex-wife Victoria Horgan into the flat and shot her in the head with a shotgun in front of her two young children. He shot both her sister, Emma Walton, and their mother,

Jacqueline Bailey, in the upper body. He then ran off to commit suicide the following day, in Peterborough.

A neighbour, Roy Gibson, called the emergency services. The ambulance arrived at the police rendezvous within three minutes of being called but paramedics were not allowed by the police to act. The women lay bleeding (dying, as it turned out) as the emergency services stood off from the crime scene waiting for a risk assessment to be carried out. It took over an hour. A helicopter was dispatched to see whether the gunman was still in the area.

An increasingly desperate Mr Gibson called the police six times. But his assurances that the gunman had run off weren't taken seriously. The gunman might still be on the scene making him say these things, the police reasoned, to lure them into a trap. The officer in charge of the operation wouldn't let the paramedics into the area to help the women for health and safety reasons.

'Vicky and Emma could have been saved if the paramedics had been allowed to the scene,' Mr Gibson said.

A spokesman for Royal Berkshire Ambulance Service said, 'In a situation such as this, it is vital that the scene is confirmed as being safe to enter. Reports indicated that the attacker was still on the scene and that the situation remained very dangerous.' The situation was most dangerous for the women who were in the process of bleeding to death while officers waited for a risk assessment to be completed.

Mr Gibson, who was 70 at the time of the killings, stood guard outside while his wife tended to the wounded women. 'My wife's inside the house; I'm outside the house with a lump of wood in my hand just in case he did come back. But it didn't matter to me if he had come back. We weren't scared. We did what human beings are supposed to do. There's three people lying in that house bleeding to death. These are neighbours, friends; you're supposed to help.'

Mr Gibson's wife Georgina, 58, an amateur first-aider, struggled to save Mrs Horgan. She couldn't do it. She bled to death, leaving behind her daughters, aged three and seven. 'I was a St John Ambulancer,' Mrs Gibson said. 'I used those skills as much as I could. It was difficult because I couldn't move her. I tried to tell her to hang in there for the kids. But I was just running from one to the other – the three were all bleeding.'

Mr Gibson said, 'My wife was trying to administer first aid to Victoria and the other two, but couldn't save them. There was blood everywhere. It was carnage.

'We don't think Vicky would have survived. She didn't survive: she died while we were there. I don't know about Emma. I think she virtually bled to death. Whether she could have been helped or not, I don't know. But it seems a bit stupid to leave it nearly an hour and a half before you find out.' He says he has never had a bad word to say about the police, and he isn't having a go at them now. 'All I'm trying to say is that the system can't be right if it leaves three people like that who have been shot.'

The area commander defended the lack of action in these terms: 'Firearms operations demand a calculated response to safeguard any members of the public who could be at risk as well as officers and other emergency service personnel. We had reports indicating that the assailant was still at the scene and that the situation remained very dangerous. For all we knew he could have been hiding behind a fence nearby.'

Had the health-and-safety protocols been ignored, the officer in charge might have sent in police and paramedics. Had the gunman still been there ('hiding behind a fence'), and had that hiding gunman shot any of the public servants, there would have been very large sums in legal fees and compensation to be paid. The officer in charge weighed the remote possibility of a gunman's luring them into a trap against the virtual certainty of injury or death to three bleeding women.

Had this been a question of the safety of the public, the decision would have been made to send in the officers. If it was more a question of the safety of public servants, and reinforced by anti-compensation proto-cols, then it was entirely correct.

It was hardly conducive to public health or safety after all: three women bled to death as their friends pleaded for help.

By the rarest chance, in 2005 a government minister witnessed this standard procedure first-hand. David Lammy – a constitutional affairs minister at the time, and responsible for the criminal justice system – was visiting a Broadwater Farm community centre, London, for an embassy reception. Masked gunman drove by and opened fire into the crowd, hitting one Charles Oseibonsu in the body.

The minister – to his credit – stayed on the scene and tried to stop the blood flow from the boy's shoulder. Police and paramedics arrived at the scene promptly but stood off a few hundred yards from the boy, refusing to approach closer. Mr Lammy jumped in his car and drove up to the police to get them into action. They wouldn't budge. They were making a risk assessment.

The police got the call at 12.04 and were on the scene in eight minutes. The London ambulance service arrived four minutes later. A further 20 minutes elapsed before the paramedics were allowed to attend the boy.

'I am demanding answers from the police as to why they arrived on scene, stopped short and waited while a boy lay bleeding from a gunshot wound ... He was in incredible agony, screaming in pain, drifting in and out of consciousness.'

John Mensah, chairman of the Haringey Ghanaian Community group, which organised the event, said,

'The police response was not acceptable. There can be no excuses.'

If there were no cost-and-compensation implications, if it were purely a matter of personal and public safety, it is very unlikely officers would stand back from bleeding citizens while a government minister railed at them to come and help.

It's not a question of personal bravery. They have the guts, these men and women, as Julia Drown pointed out in March 2006, in the House of Commons:

'When Julia [Pemberton] heard sounds of commotion outside, she called the police. Her 16-minute 999 call described her fear for her and her son's lives. She reported several gunshots and pleaded for help. The transcript, read out at the inquest, left out crucial parts of the call. During the call, Julia was asked repeatedly to give her address. She sought advice on whether to run or stay, and was told to stay hidden. She questioned why it was taking the police so long to arrive, and was told that police were on their way "now". Perhaps a minute before she died, she was even led to believe that they were outside the house. She was told to stop screaming and shouting.

'Julia was asked to give directions to her house. It took between 10 and 12 minutes before the property was identified, despite the fact that it was flagged on the police computer and that previously Julia had been told that even a silent 999 call would be responded to urgently. It is sickening to think of how Julia must have felt when it dawned on her – as it clearly did – that, despite repeated police promises of a fast response if she ever rang 999, they did not even know where she lived.

'Of course, Julia was not allowed to know that the firearms policy at the time appeared to exclude the option of immediate attendance to firearms incidents. We have heard differing police dispatch times. The first response was unarmed, and left 24 minutes – not, as she had been led to expect, 10 minutes – from the start of the call. It took 24 minutes for an unarmed team to be dispatched. By then, William had been shot five times, and Julia four times.

'That unarmed team dispatched to locate the property arrived to see William's body on the drive. In an incredible act of bravery, and contrary to Thames Valley police policy, the three officers – Hadley, Ainsley and Blackburn – attempted to help William. The family have thanked those officers and I join them. However, the irony is that the officers who stand out as having done everything, and more, that the family could have expected from the police were the ones who breached the police's policy.'

Gloucester Crown Court was told that David Collinson had been woken by the noise of a fire and, thinking burglars were in his Cheltenham building, had gone to investigate, taking an imitation gun. Once outside his second-floor flat, he found three police officers, who had tried to get everyone out of the building but had been beaten back by thick smoke.

Collinson received a call on his mobile telephone from his terrified wife, still inside. As he tried to go back in, the officers stopped him. They weren't prepared to go in, but he was. He produced the imitation gun, pointed it at them and ran inside to rescue his wife and their dog. Afterwards he apologised to the officers.'

The police who tried to stop brave Mr Collinson were operating within the logic of their law. Had they let him go back into the building and he'd been injured, the police could have been sued for not forcibly restraining him (remember the Gaping Ghyll case in Chapter 2).

So, the man saved his wife from burning to death and, instead of getting a medal for bravery, was charged with threatening the police with an imitation firearm. Considering the circumstances, he was treated leniently. They sent him to prison for a year.

I seem to remember a remark of Lord Denning's. He was considering a politician's remark about the citizen's duty being to obey the law at all times. 'Piffle!' he said (I paraphrase). There are occasions when it is a citizen's duty to break the law. For instance, a husband is duty-bound to break a 30mph speed limit when he is getting his pregnant, haemorrhaging wife to the labour ward.

That view sounds very old-fashioned now. I suspect the balance of administrative opinion today would come down heavily against Lord Denning. He might even be charged with incitement.

For art's sake

Despite the fire burning in another part of his house, an 83-year-old former army officer tried to get back inside to save the paintings and possessions of a lifetime. When he was told by police he couldn't go inside he objected. They locked him in their police van until his house and everything in it had burned down.

He said in court, 'It was my right as a property owner to make my own choice. The fire broke out in the boiler house in the rear of the property. I dialled 999 and my wife and I thought we ought to take the pictures down.

'We are in our eighties and have collected these things over the course of a lifetime. They go back three generations. We went to the drawing room and dining room and there was plenty of time. The house wasn't smoke-logged. I'm not someone who will stand around and watch things happen.'

Captain Carlisle said two constables arrived as he started to remove the paintings. 'They demanded we leave the house and I said, "Don't be bloody stupid." There were three oak doors between us and the fire.

'I was seized and hauled out. I struggled, but it is not in my nature to lose my temper. I was overpowered and taken out. After about 20 minutes I was put in a police van. I was thrown into a small cage in the back.

'The police say they were trying to save my life, which is rubbish. There was no possible risk. The fire took 90 minutes to get across the house. Meanwhile, all our possessions could have been saved.'

He was trying to sue the Dyfed Powys Police for false imprisonment; the police tried to get the action struck out. At time of going to press the issue was unresolved.

How Not to Drown

There's something about swimming in rivers, lakes and quarries that brings out the worst in our officers, officials and public service supervisors. They don't like it one little bit. It's almost coming down to a test of wills between a firm government and a disobedient public.

The British official attitude, as issued by the government's own Water Safety Forum, says:

'Even during the warmer summer months in the UK inland waters remain cold. However, as the air temperature rises, people are increasingly likely to jump or dive into lakes and rivers to cool off. Research has shown that many will be able to swim, the majority of them will be male, and alcohol and/or peer pressure may feature in their decision to plunge in. As a result of sudden immersion in cold water, hidden currents and submerged hazards like refuse and vegetation, many will get into difficulties and be unable to save themselves. For these reasons the Forum says DO NOT SWIM AT UNSUPERVISED INLAND WATER SITES.'

Just to emphasise that: The Water Safety Forum says, in bold capitals, that no one, whether or not they are male, or subject to peer pressure or influenced by alcohol, should go swimming in a river unless they are supervised (presumably by a lifeguard who has got his NVQ in lifesaving).

They also say that, although 'many' who do go in will be swimmers, 'many will be unable to save themselves' unless they swim under the gaze of a lifeguard.

That leaves many of us in a difficulty. What of those of us who like swimming without being watched over? What if we like lying on our back in a slowly moving Thames looking at the clouds and listening to the sound of fertiliser slowly dripping into the water? What if we like discreetly taking our clothes off and swimming without swimming trunks without supervision? ASBOs are probably the answer.

There's a lovely natural park at Brereton Heath in southeast Cheshire. It has a delicious, 14-acre, tree-lined lake with sandy beach access to the water. It's popular with the public, visited by many tens of thousands of people a year. People swim, no matter how much they are discouraged by the official policy. Almost no accidents happen there, and the handful that do require brief medical attention.

All bar one, in recent times. It was the site of a paralysis some years ago, when a young man dived in too steeply and hit his head on the bottom. 'I do not think,' said Lord Hoffman, when the case got to the

House of Lords, 'that the [council's] legal duty to the claimant in the circumstances required them to take the extreme measures which were completed after the accident.'

Anyway, the council's countryside manager prepared a paper. He described how popular the park had become: 'The total number of visitors now exceeds 160,000 per annum ... The lake acts as a magnet to the public and has become heavily used for swimming in spite of a no-swimming policy due to safety considerations ... Advice has been sought from the County Council's Water Safety Officer as to how the problem should be addressed and this has been carefully followed. Notices are posted warning of the dangers and leaflets are handed to visitors to emphasise the situation. Life belts and throwing lines are provided for use in emergencies.

'In spite of these actions the public continue to ignore the advice and the requests of the rangers not to swim. The attitude is that they will do what they want to do and that rangers should not interfere with their enjoyment. There have been several occasions when small children have been out in the middle of the lake and their parents have been extremely rude to staff when approached about this.

'As a result of the general flaunting of the policy there have been a number of near fatalities in the lake with three incidents requiring hospital treatment in the week around Whitsun. Whilst the rangers are doing all they can to protect the public it is likely to be only a matter of time before someone drowns.'

NB: Weil's disease is a life-threatening infection often used to justify swimming bans. There are, according to Medicdirect, around 70 cases of Weil's disease a year in Britain and five fatalities. Weil's disease is said to occur in 10 per cent of cases and causes severe complications but ... the risks, in short, are insignificant.

The Borough Council's leisure officer visited the park and concluded that the notices and leaflets were not having the desired effect. Further action was taken in hand:

'I want the water's edge to be far less accessible, desirable and inviting than it currently is for children's beach/water's edge type of play activities. I personally find this course of action a regrettable one but I have to remind myself that Council policy was to establish a Country Park and not specifically to provide a swimming facility, no matter how popular this may have become in consequence.

'To provide a facility that is open to the public and which contains beach and water areas is, in my view, an open invitation and temptation to swim and engage in other water's edge activities despite the cautionary note that is struck by deterrent notices etc., and in that type of situation accidents become inevitable.

'We must therefore do everything that is reasonably possible to deter, discourage and prevent people from swimming or paddling in the lake or diving into the lake ... Work should be prepared for the report with a view to implementation of a scheme at the earliest opportunity, bearing in mind that we shall require a supplementary estimate for the exercise.'

The swimmers strike back

There's a great little organisation with a website called www.river-swimming.co.uk who – true to their name – support swimming in rivers and issue their own statistical crunch of the figures. The official safety spokespeople tend to say there are 450 drowning deaths a year and 175 drownings in rivers a year. The pro-swimmers point out that, if you exclude suicides, homicides and drunks 'jumping in', you get about 25 swimmers who drown each year in inland waterways. It's not a statistically significant number.

But river safety officers are required to look at a river in terms of safety. That's their job. That's what they're paid for. There are very few safety aspects to a river. They are, of their nature, a danger, a risk. A river, to a river safety officer, is one long, bending, sliding death trap.

How to make rivers safe is a very odd project and will lead to really jaw-dropping ideas: 'It would be impractical, in some cases impossible and in conflict with the landscape,' they say, 'to fence much of the UK's inland waters.' That's the National Water Safety Forum (who replaced the National Water Safety Committee). They want to show that they have at least considered the possibility of fencing Britain's inland waters.

But, logically, there's only one safety conclusion they can come to, and they do indeed come to it.

'The most positive way of preventing drowning is to ensure that entry into the water does not happen in the first place.'

This is the attitude underlying the official set of standards, or codes or best practices. And, if any local authorities ignore those standards, codes and best practices, they will be vulnerable in a court of law to having someone sue them. The prosecuting barrister will point out that the official standards and recommendations were ignored and flouted, and that a tragedy resulted. 'You knew the risk that you were taking!' the barrister might tell a council's represen- tative in the dock. 'You knew and you ignored it, and now this death is on your conscience! And on your balance sheet!'

*

In a widely noted case from 2005, a swimming club seeking the right to take winter swims in ponds north of London in the absence of lifeguards won a victory in the High Court against the Authority, which 'had claimed that it risked prosecution by the Health and Safety Executive if it allowed unsupervised dips'. Mr Justice

Stanley Burnton ruled that the corporation had fallen into legal error and said club members should be able to swim at their own risk. He spoke out in favour of 'individual freedom' and against the imposition of 'a grey and dull safety regime', adding that by granting permission to the club the corporation would not be liable to prosecution for breaches of health and safety.

Mary Cane, chair of the Hampstead Heath Winter Swimming Club, said. 'This was a test case with wide implications for all open swimming in England and represents another successful attack by ordinary citizens on the nanny state and the cult of health and safety.'

Ms Cane said that the club was proud to have played its part 'in re-establishing an important principle of personal freedom in this country, taken for granted everywhere else, that responsible adults must be free to decide for themselves whether to pursue recreational activities involving an element of risk.'

But, if you think that is the matter resolved in favour of freedom, nationwide, you must think again. There are thousands of officials out there whose contracts require them to implement stringent safety regimes. They are not people who like saying, 'My work is done, my job is useless, I am now going to train to be a gardener.' No, these people belong to the government and you cannot get rid of them. They're like luggage.

If you are interested in the machinery of government, try penetrating this lot:

'The National Water Safety Foundation engenders links with the Maritime Safety Coordinating Committee and the UK Search and Rescue Strategic Committee. Each of these groups works closely with the new inter-departmental Government Group.

'The National Water Safety Forum has allowed greater participation by organisations with an interest in water safety by creating six advisory groups: Beach Safety, Inland Water Safety, Sea Safety, Swimming Pool Safety, Water Sports Safety and an Information Group. Members of each group meet to discuss issues relevant to their topic and field of expertise and develop policy and guidance. The chair of each advisory group sits on the Coordinating Group, which is the overall steering group of the Forum and provides the link with the Inter-Departmental Government Group ...'

This is all going only one way. None of these people are going to report back that there is an excess of safety measures.

All their recommendations and draft regulations and best-practice roll-out form the basis of widespread action by public bodies fearful of these standards or codes or pronouncements that create a culture of thought.

Because, whatever they say at the top of these organisations, their influence spreads out in ways they can't predict or control. So, although the head of the Health and Safety Executive may say he's in favour of something like the Bude tidal pool in North Cornwall, local safety officers and safety advisers and consultants – who all have jobs to do and livings to make – are the people who make the actual decisions on these matters.

In the case of the Bude tidal pool, they read the Blue Book. It's a set of guidelines for swimming pools. As these are the only guidelines available, they are applied to outdoor swimming as well. But when you conduct a risk assessment of a tidal pool you find that the standards found there do not conform to the standards required of swimming pools. Water clarity is below that of the municipal pool. There are slippery surfaces and there are no provisions for keeping the public out when the pool is not officially open.

The river swimmers say: 'Not surprisingly, the North Cornwall District Council, intimidated by the risk of prosecution by the Health and Safety Executive and allegedly acting on the advice of the HSE and an independent health and safety adviser, closed the pool at the beginning of the 2004 season. Following an eruption of public anger they entered into a process of consultations and later re-opened the pool for the remainder of the season under the supervision of a small army of lifeguards.'

The river swimmers' sensible proposition is this: 'In our opinion, sea pools should be evaluated in their context ("safer than the sea and therefore to be encouraged") rather than in absolute terms (i.e. "unsafe") thus ignoring the fact that if a sea pool goes, people are more likely to use the less-safe sea.

Obviously, closing sea pools promotes neither the health nor the safety of the public.'

The Bude tidal pool has been reprieved. But what energy, what anger had to be deployed against the officials so that an ordinary, traditional safety practice could continue.

How to be a Victim

The rules of correct behaviour in this culture are the most annoying thing about it. To get damages in this country, unlike America, you still have to prove you've been damaged. Luckily, doctors and the courts will often accept your estimation of how much you've been damaged. If they have video footage of you playing a violent contact sport while you are claiming not be able to walk more than six feet without sitting down, you will say, 'You caught me on a good day.'

The more you look and sound damaged, the better you will do. And the best way to look and sound damaged is to feel it.

The following include a number of important phrases you should include in your deposition.

- 'I nearly suffered a nervous breakdown.' Or better still, 'I suffered a nervous breakdown.'

- 'I am taking antidepressants and suffer constant flashbacks and nightmares.'

- 'He was bullying me and I felt scared, so words were my only way to fight back. I felt cornered and powerless.' Extra points for 'powerless'!

- 'He was extremely frightening and intimidating. When I left the restaurant I began to suffer depression and anxiety. I now see men completely differently.'

- 'I wouldn't call what I have a life – I just exist.'

- 'As a result, I suffered a nervous breakdown and developed severe clinical depression. Basically, I wanted to commit suicide. I thought about crashing my car.'

- 'I was unable to distinguish my dreams, which were solely about work, from reality.'

- 'They have made me very ill with stress and depression and my home life has suffered as a result.'

- 'The memories of the accident have caused such mental scarring that I am now frightened of being transported in any form. Even a car. But especially by train. I cannot be near a train. I cannot look at a train. And the sound of one causes dizziness and sweating.' (Substitute 'vacuum cleaner' for 'train', if the accident in question involved a vacuum cleaner.)

The victim's instruction manual

Going more deeply into the practicalities of constructing your case for damages, here is a very useful document from a law firm, Baron and Budd, in the United States. They specialise in asbestosis claims, but the thinking can be applied to many different sorts of ailment. The document coaches clients for their court appearance.

The punctuation and emphases are in the original; the full text can be found at http://www.aei.org/research/liability/subjectAreas/pageID.1006,projectID.23/default.asp

'It is very IMPORTANT that you give concrete examples of how your life has been "damaged" ...

'SHORTNESS OF BREATH. Think about it. There are very few things in life which are not affected by your ability to breathe ... be thinking about all the activities you have given up or must do more slowly because of shortness of breath. Some examples might be:

- Do you have difficulty sleeping at night because it is difficult to breathe lying down?
- Do you sleep propped up with pillows or sitting up in a chair to breathe easier?
- Do you wake frequently at night to cough or do you wake up in the morning coughing?
- Has your sex life been affected by shortness of breath?
- Do you take medications for breathing or anxiety or any other health problem? Bring ALL your medications along with you to the deposition so the

Court recorder can type the names onto the record, even if you don't take the medications regularly.

'WORK:

- Did you have to retire early because you could not keep up with the other workers your age?

- Have you turned down any overtime? Be thinking about how much money you have lost by having to refuse overtime, retire early or take a lower-paying job.

'HOUSEHOLD MAINTENANCE

- Do you pay someone else to mow your yard? If so, how much do you pay? Did you purchase a rider-mower because you just couldn't use a push mower any more?

- Have you given up growing a vegetable garden? How big did your garden used [sic] to be? How big is it now? Have you lost any money by not being able to sell the extra produce?

- Did you pay SOMEONE ELSE to do household repairs such as plumbing, electrical and roof repairs? Did you have gas heat installed because you could no longer cut firewood? Did you have aluminum siding put on because you don't have the energy to paint any more?

'HOBBIES

'The hobbies you once enjoyed gave meaning to your life. You worked all your life looking forward to retirement so you could enjoy them!

- Have you given up or cut down on hunting, fishing, camping, boating, softball, golfing, travel, raising animals or any other activities? Name as many as you can think of.

'FAMILY

'Your relationship with your family is one of your greatest joys in life.

- Are you spending less time with young children or grandchildren because they make you too tired or irritable?
- Would your spouse and other relatives say that you are short-tempered or easily frustrated because you are not able to do the things you once enjoyed?'

Do you want fries with your rat?

Obviously the sort of training above works, since depositions often bear a certain family resemblance.

Here is part of a claim in the Ontario Superior Court of Justice. Noora Mohamad's little daughter Ayan found part of a rat's head in her Big Mac. Obviously, a normal life was no longer possible for anyone involved. The mother wanted the following.

- For the directly affected child, general damages of $2 million, special damages of $100,000 and punitive, exemplary and aggravated damages of $5 million.

- For the mother herself, the same amounts (with a $50,000 reduction in the special damages just to show this has been carefully thought through).

- For the little girl's little sister, general and special damages of just $100,000 combined. This is a reasonable claim after all. There's no need to go overboard. The rat's head wasn't actually hers. But, then again, she was a witness to the holocaust so she should, on reflection, get her own punitive damages of $5 million.

Here is a description (taken from the court deposition that Mrs Mohamad's lawyer put in) of the actual damage that would be soothed, smoothed and assuaged by the application of £17 million:

'Ayan was assessed by a psychologist and has undergone psychotherapy. She has been diagnosed as suffering from a separation anxiety disorder, features of post-traumatic stress disorder and an acute adjustment disorder with mixed anxiety and depressed mood. More specifically, she has suffered psychiatric damages, including:

a) phobias concerning certain types of foods, and eating outside of her home

b) persistent sensations of feeling hairs in her mouth

c) fear of sleeping and using the washroom alone

d) sleep disturbances and nightmares

e) flashbacks

f) overly attached to her mother

g) chronic anxiety, with physical symptoms including vomiting and stomach pains

h) feelings of betrayal and inability to trust others

i) decreased social activity

j) panic-like sensations

'The said injuries were accompanied by great pain and suffering. She has received a severe physical and emotional shock to her system and will be permanently injured thereby. She has suffered from traumatic, emotional and nervous upset and has lost the enjoyment of life. She has been unable to carry on with her normal tasks of living.'

On and on it goes. The mother also received 'a severe physical and emotional shock and will be permanently injured thereby. She has suffered from traumatic, emotional and nervous upset and has lost the enjoyment of life ...' And so on. Copy and paste for the other daughter who saw her sister and the rat. She is suffering from the same psychological damage, but her prognosis is better than her sister's. 'She *may* continue to suffer from the effects of her injuries for the rest of her life.'

On their own account, this highly strung family have been psychologically destroyed by an unpleasant episode. But it's worth considering whether the therapeutic aftermath was more damaging than the experience. If the child was so susceptible to a rat, it is more than likely that a skilful therapist could amplify those symptoms simply by focusing on them. It is essential for the case, after all, that these symptoms don't disappear. For the big money, the damage has to be long-lasting. Permanent, indeed.

So, the incentive for the relatives, especially the mother, is to keep the damage well to the fore. Thus, the morning scene in their psychologically destroyed household may go like this.

'Oh, good morning, darling, my angel. And how is your rat terror this morning?'

'Not too bad, Mama, actually, I think it's getting better.'

'Brave child! But be careful not to put yourself into denial. And if you didn't dream of rats in your hamburger again, did you dream of rats in your bed, under your pillow, biting their way through to eat into your brain through your ears?'

'I must say, Mama, that the fear is fading day by day. This morning it seems 24 hours more remote than it did yesterday.'

'Do be careful not to damage yourself any further by suppressing your horror and disgust and slimy revulsion at the filthy rat experience, my little mouse. You must come to terms with your feelings at the prickly little black rat hairs in your *mouth* and to see its nasty little teeth with all their billions of rat bacteria springing down your throat to multiply and mutate, and breed more rat bacteria in your *stomach*, and the dead rat's eye gazing malevolently as you chew its crunchy little bones wondering every time you put your hand into your pocket you'll find a *rat* there, or your little toes into your boots there'll be a *rat* there. But let me get you a lovely bowl of Cheerios, which I have checked to make sure there aren't any *rats* in the packet ... Arrrrrrggggggrghh! Argh! Argh! A rat! A *rat*! *A RAT!* Oh, no, it's not: it's your socks. Sorry, my darling, *fetch the sick bowl*! I was just overcome with terror at the thought of losing the $17 million.'

Stupid joke. Apologies all round.

Research suggests that these injuries – if they exist, and even if they were caused by the therapist, or by the mother herself – are unlikely to be healed while this lawsuit is extant. When the lawsuit is dismissed, the child's symptoms will disappear, like dew in the morning sun. But, while the case remains pending, the child must keep the symptoms going if she's to have any chance of a share in the $17 million.

An unsuitable case for treatment ...

The power of the mind seems to be as important as – and frequently more important than – the physical treatment offered, in terms of recuperation.

Here's the experience of the wife of a man who survived the Piper Alpha drilling-rig disaster in Britain in 1988, when an explosion destroyed an oil-production platform, killing 167 people. He had as much (if not more) difficulty surviving the subsequent counselling.

Margaret MacFarlane (wife of Frank) went to her husband's counselling service to give them a piece of her mind. She told a documentary team how the meeting had gone. She'd said, 'Do you know that when he comes home after your sessions the world revolves around him? I work the other hours of the day to make him feel normal, and to try and build up his resilience to all the knocks and problems life presents, and he comes back from your sessions feeling "Woe is me". And they said, "We'll give you some counselling." '

Mastermind, eat your heart out!

Whenever you go to law you throw yourself into the hazard. The outcome is unpredictable. And, goodness knows, the input can be pretty odd, too.

Here's a quiz from *Personnel Today*:

1. The courts refused to hear the sex-discrimination claim of a female associate of the Church of Scotland because:

   a) At the preliminary hearing she maintained that her legal representative was God

   b) She was a vexatious litigant

   c) Her employer is God

   d) She requested that the tribunal assemble in Church

2. A mortuary technician was unfairly dismissed after she developed a morbid fear of:

   a) Enclosed spaces

   b) The dark

   c) Ghosts

   d) Death

3. An apprentice plumber claimed sex discrimination after his employer:

   a) Insisted on several occasions that the apprentice accompany him to a lap dancing club

   b) Beat him with an 'apprentice correction stick'

   c) Insisted that the apprentice purchase 'top shelf' magazines for him

   d) Refused to let him wear a coat over his overalls in winter

4. A train driver was awarded damages for psychological injury after:

   a) The brakes on his train failed

   b) He was attacked by an irate commuter

   c) His train struck and killed a goat

   d) He suffered a campaign of practical jokes at the hands of a ticket collector

5. An airline masseuse was awarded £109,000 in compensation because:

   a) She broke her arm during turbulence

   b) She developed a fear of flying which led to her dismissal

c) She developed Repetitive Strain Injury

d) She was sexually harassed by an air steward

ANSWERS

1) c – Helen Percy was suspended from her job when, as a single woman, she was accused of having sex with a married Church elder. She resigned and alleged that she had been discriminated against because the Kirk had 'not taken similar action against male ministers who are known to have had/are still having extramarital sexual relationships'. The Church of Scotland Act 1921 says that the Church receives from 'the Lord Jesus Christ, its Divine King and Head' the right and power 'subject to no civil authority to legislate, and to adjudicate finally, in all matters of doctrine, worship and government, and discipline in the Church, including the right to determine all questions concerning membership and office in the Church'. The House of Lords is to determine who Percy's employer is.

2) d – Mrs Capener, the mortuary assistant, was awarded £15,000 in compensation for unfair dismissal, damages and injury to her feelings and loss of statutory rights. Mrs Capener had worked in the same mortuary for 21 years, which left her with symptoms of clinical depression and post-traumatic stress disorder. She was signed off sick in January 2004. Because her employer failed to redeploy her and because her illness prevented her from returning to work, she was effectively dismissed.

3) b – The employee argued at the Employment Appeal Tribunal that the employer had treated him less favourably than a hypothetical female apprentice, since the employer had admitted in evidence that, bar a clip round the ear, he would not hit a woman or treat a woman in the same way as the employee alleged he had been treated. The tribunal found that the employee had been discriminated against on the grounds of sex.

4) c – The train driver received £35,000 as compensation for the shock and trauma and subsequent loss of pension. Railtrack (now Network Rail) admitted liability for the incident, caused by broken fencing between Weymouth and Waterloo.

5) c – Elizabeth King sued Virgin Atlantic when she had to give up her £19,000-a-year post at Heathrow airport because she had developed repetitive-strain injury (RSI) through giving passengers massages. A doctor commented that he believed the RSI was caused by the large number of shiatsu massages and the abnormal position her clients were in when she performed them. The court ordered Virgin Atlantic to pay compensation for loss of earnings, pain and suffering.

Stella Liebeck: The hot-coffee case

She is the international compensation icon. You've heard of her. She is cited by both sides of the argument. This is the conclusive summary for and against. There is much said on both sides.

Vanessa Feltz, writing in her *Daily Star* column some years ago, said, 'We live in a compensation culture. Everyone's running scared of litigation. Terror of being sued means it's only minutes until pavements are painted with gigantic government warnings in case we catch our stilettoes in a crack and sue the local council. And overpaid café lattes will carry huge labels lest you burn your tongue and slap a writ on them like the American plonker who gulped her McDonald's coffee and took Ronald McD to the cleaners.'

Sir David Arculus, chairman of the Better Regulation Task Force (BRTF), makes the opposite case: 'The truth about this "American plonker",' he said, 'is starkly different.'

Sir David (he says 'the compensation culture is a damaging myth') makes it all sound so reasonable.

He continues, 'Stella Liebeck (79) was trying to add cream to her coffee while she was a passenger in a stationary car. The spillage was her fault but she could not have expected the consequences:

- the coffee was served at 88°C (190°F). Any temperature above 65°C (149°F) will cause serious burns;

- there had been 700 prior complaints against this superheated coffee;

'Further, McDonald's:

- knew of the risk of severe burns from its coffee;

- decided not to warn customers of the risk despite knowing most of their customers would not recognise it;
- knew its coffee was not fit for consumption as served; and
- did not intend to change its policies in the light of the evidence at trial.

'Although hospitalised for 8 days and disabled for 2 years with third-degree burns, Mrs Liebeck did not want to litigate but McDonald's refused to refund her $10,000 medical expenses;

'The jury awarded $200,000 compensatory damages and $2.7 million punitive damages. The court reduced this to $160,000 and $480,000 respectively. Under these circumstances few would object to the injured woman having a right to claim for damages.'

Few would object? What a suave, mandarin way of presenting a highly tendentious – and ultimately ridiculous – proposition.

Mrs Liebeck received half a million dollars for a self-inflicted wound from coffee served at the recommended temperature. Yes, the recommended temperature! (Every detail of this story is twisted one way or the other.) Stella supporters say McDonald's coffee served at just 165 degrees Fahrenheit is 'superheated' – the company is deliberately and recklessly serving dangerously hot coffee. However, the National Coffee Association recommends brewing coffee at 205 degrees

Fahrenheit and that it be maintained at 180–5 degrees Fahrenheit. That's the industry standard for hot coffee. That's what hot coffee is. That's how customers like to drink it.

Returning to the story, she was 'disabled for 2 years'. That isn't quite true: she *had treatment* for two years. She was disabled for two years only insofar as she couldn't have got a job rolling Cuban cigars on her thighs for two years.

Did she offer to settle for $10,000? The tort-reform website Overlawyered.com says she initially asked for $20,000. 'And why should McDonald's offer any money when they hadn't done anything wrong?' they ask.

There had been '700 prior complaints'? Yes. True. Correct. Over ten years there were 700 cases of heat damage to consumers drinking McDonald's coffee. Some accidents were mild, some serious. But that accident rate represents one accident per 24 million cups of coffee sold by McDonald's. Is that 'wilful, wanton, reckless or malicious conduct' by the company? Should 24 million cups of coffee be reduced in temperature to something approaching tepid to prevent one (possibly minor) injury?

This is getting theological. Cardinal Newman said it would be better that the whole human race be damned for eternity than a child tell one white lie. That's the sort of otherworldly logic that is being applied to these sorts of public safety issues.

Mind you, aren't McDonald's cups built a little more sturdily than they used to be? Is that worth half a million dollars? The selfish fact is I didn't have to pay it, and it all happened a long way away.

The Case ~~for~~ the Denial

Everyone has an agenda in this area. It is intensely political. You don't know what you're hearing until you know who's speaking. That's how you know it's political.

This is how they line up:

Personal injury lawyers, most trades unions, the government, the *Guardian*, the Left say: there is no compensation culture. At most there is a *perception* of a compensation culture, which has a regrettable effect, but this is more than outweighed by the access to the justice system for people without means.

The Right, many insurance companies, solicitors who defend companies, doctors, businesspeople, quite a lot of local authorities in their quiet way, teachers, some teaching unions, small-business owners and the government (because they like to cover all sides of an argument, just in case) say: the compensation culture exists, costs us all dear, is eating away at notions of personal responsibility and creating a client class of victims.

If the preceding information has failed to make the case, consider this lot.

The Chief Medical Officer tells us that the estimated annual value of medical compensation in 1975 was £1 million (about £7 million in today's money). Last year the NHS paid out over £500 million.

And, underneath that, 60 to 70 per cent of claims never get beyond initial contact with a solicitor or disclosure of medical records. Of those that do proceed, 95 per cent of the claims settled by the NHS legal unit to September 2002 were settled out of court.

The Compensation Recovery Unit figures show that, in four of the last five years, new personal-injury claims have numbered in excess of 700,000. In 2000 it was estimated that 30 per cent of people with a reasonable claim for compensation actually pursued the case. By 2003, that number had risen to 66 per cent. Now, research from the Norwich Union suggests that nearly everyone says they are more likely to make a claim than they might have been a decade earlier.

And yet those who would deny that we have a compensation culture point out that the number of claims fell by 10 and 20 per cent over the last two and three years. The number of court payouts has fallen, it is true (though the value of them has risen). But, then again, the last IUA/ABI study, published in March 2003, analysed over a million motor personal-injury claims. (It is the biggest exercise of its kind ever undertaken, covering more than 90 per cent of the UK insurance market.)

It concluded that the cost of bodily-injury claims rose by nearly 10 per cent per year over the period 1991–2001.

How can all these sets of figures be right? There is no central record of the number of claims settled out of court or cases decided in chambers where a judge makes an order essentially in private.

So who knows what level the litigation is running at? Answer: nobody.

All these figures conceal as much as they reveal. High Court civil cases, for instance, fell from nearly 20,000 in 1988 to just over 4,000 a decade later. But most of the (marvellously increased) litigation was transferred into court-linked arbitration and mediation schemes. Private sector settlements may not even be collated at all.

As for out-of-court settlements, they're even less available. It is often cheaper for companies to settle small claims with an 'eff-off' payment (that's a technical term) than to go through the process. They also want to keep their liabilities quiet (which is why most settlements have a confidentiality clause written into them). As a result, companies large and small live with a permanent threat of blackmail for various infringements of various protocols – health and safety (to enrage the Right), or free speech (to anger the Left).

The 2004 Better Regulation Task Force investigation is frequently quoted as the final word. It's a government document, but it still carries weight. It was authored by the Taskforce's chairman, Sir David Arculus, whose magical name adds a weird, otherworldly authority to it.

But, because it is a government document, it has to perform to a political brief. Very often, political briefs from the Big Tent of Blairism require people to say a thing and its opposite. As a result, the Task Force document is a delicious example of its kind.

In their opening argument, in the chapter entitled 'The compensation culture: it's all in the mind', the BRTF declare, 'Almost everyone we spoke to in the course of this study told us that they did not believe that there is a compensation culture in the UK.'

When you consider how many people actually *do* believe there is a compensation culture in the UK, it is odd, you may think, that they couldn't find anyone to tell them their view. He could have started with the risk-management company Aon, the Scouts, the Guides, the Royal Aero Club, the English Outdoor Council, Volunteering England, Sport England and the Central Council of Physical Recreation – *and* the Parliamentary All-Party Group on Adventure and Recreation in Society, right there in Westminster.

But this is a technique of the modern administration. Tony Blair used it a lot to invade Iraq. If you have decided on a course of action, it is essential you do not hear evidence against your case. If you don't hear it, you can't be accused of ignoring it.

The second half of the BRTF's opening argument is equally suspect. A compensation culture can't exist, they say, because 'the number of personal injury claims is going down'. This is said time and again by the pro-compensation camp.

It's entirely possible there has been a reduction in the last two or three years. But it's a small reduction off a vast generational increase.

And it's also true that the amount of legal activity is impossible to gauge. Maybe it is actually going down, maybe it isn't. There is no central register or database of claims, cases are brought in many different tribunals and courts, and an unknowable number of cases get settled before they appear in any formal adjudication. The Chief Medical Officer, for instance, tells us that 95 per cent of cases against the NHS fail very quickly, around the time of disclosure.

Ninety-five per cent! What a bubbling pot of discontent *that* represents! It is amazing (and admirable of persons unknown) that these discontents are being kept under control somehow or other (an apology would do the trick, in a third of cases, it turns out).

So we can agree that the legal system is working well to defend society from (shall we call it?) a compensation subculture — one that would entirely disable and dismantle a public health service if it found expression in the courts.

But who knows how many of these claims get settled by way of payments. Aggrieved employees or citizens conceive a case against someone else. Probably someone with money. They threaten to go to law. The other party realise that to defend the case will cost five times what's being asked; sometimes they make a calculated decision to pay off the complainant. Those figures don't show up anywhere in any systematic way.

While saying forcefully that the idea of a compensation culture is a myth, the Better Regulation report goes on to give cogent examples that a compensation culture exists and is damaging society. They refer to a council they know that was due to spend £2 million of its £22 million budget handling claims for compensation. The report says, 'Multiply that by all the local authorities and councils are spending a staggering amount of money each year dealing with compensation claims.' 'Many' of which 'may be spurious', it con-cludes. In other words, they agree the compensation culture is alive, well and costing billions.

It reinforces this view with the words, 'There is undoubtedly a perception that the public have a greater tendency now than ever before to seek redress if they suffer an injustice or injury, which they believe was someone else's fault. People look for someone else to blame for their misfortune.'

And finally they go on to recommend a slew of regulations and proposals to improve the situation (that is a myth). They call for legislation to change a situation that doesn't exist. As the TUC say (and they *really* don't believe a compensation culture exists), 'This is illogical.'

Nick Cohen of the *Observer* remarked on the Compensation Bill, 'His lordship is in the ridiculous position of a man who assures his wife he's not having an affair by promising to give up his mistress. He is determined to tackle a problem that doesn't exist.'

Myths and Manipulations

Those who are disposed to reject the idea of a compensation culture can do so comfortably if they angle their gaze in a certain direction to avoid the peripheral view. They can also create a good deal of diversionary activity by concentrating on the misrepresentations out there. These are multitudinous. When the media run compensation stories, they exclude all the mitigating circumstances they can. There are, in addition, a number of outright fakes in circulation. They can be detailed, named, dated, sourced, persuasive – but entirely fabricated. Here are some of the most famous.

'PHILADELPHIA, Pa. – A woman is suing the pharmacy that sold her a popular contraceptive jelly – because she ate the stuff on toast and got pregnant anyway.

'And, incredibly, many legal experts are saying she's got an excellent chance of collecting! "The woman is a complete idiot," said one attorney, who asked that we not use his name. "How bright can you be if you think eating a vaginal gel will prevent conception?

' "But certain aspects of the case involve truth in labelling and false advertising issues. She may not collect but she'll make a lot of noise and trouble. People are down on lawyers anyway. They think we waste time and money on frivolous lawsuits. This isn't going to help our public relations any."

'A spokesman for the unnamed mom-and-pop drugstore says he's shocked and angry that such a case could ever be taken seriously. "All she has to do is open the box and read the directions," says the spokesman. "Next thing you know someone will come after us because they couldn't stick things together with their toothpaste.

' "I can just imagine some moron saying: 'It's paste, isn't it? Why can't I glue these papers onto my bulletin board?'

' "But attorneys for Mrs. Chyton say she was swindled and lied to by implication and they intend to make the pharmacy pay $500,000 for the hardship the woman will have to endure.

' "It says right on it 'jelly,' " says Mrs. Chyton, a former model, who was once a cheerleader for a popular professional basketball team.

' "And they kept it on the shelf just two aisles from the food section. I know, now, that the directions say it should be used vaginally with a condom.

' "But who has time to sit around reading directions these days – especially when you're sexually aroused?

' "The company should call it something else and the pharmacy shouldn't sell it without telling each and every customer who buys it that eating it won't prevent you from getting pregnant."

'As bizarre as it sounds, the pharmacy could wind up losing the lawsuit. "It's hard for businesses to avoid troublesome lawsuits," said another attorney.

' "With the courts bending over backwards to please consumer groups, the temper of the times is perfect for these crackpots to bring legal action against businesses – even a moronic legal action like this."

Note the details, the names, the CV, the news language, the air of weary authenticity. It's all made up. Barbara and David Mikkelson (of Snopes.com) tell us: 'A brief mention of the legend (related as a 'true story') was made in an article about medication errors that appeared in the *Charleston Post and Courier* in January 1997, both Rush Limbaugh and Jay Leno reported this item as a real incident on their shows (on 6 June 1997 and 27 June 1997, respectively), and Ann Landers ran this as an example of a real 'crazy lawsuit' in her column of 5 October 1997.'

The most famous compensation myths of recent times go as follows (courtesy of the Real Stella Awards):

- 'In November, Mr. Grazinski purchased a brand new 32-foot Winnebago motor home. On his first trip home, having joined the freeway, he set the cruise control at 70 mph and calmly left the driver's seat to go into the back and make himself a cup of coffee. Not surprisingly, the Winnie left the freeway, crashed and overturned. Mr. Grazinski sued Winnebago for not advising him in the handbook that he could not actually do this. He was awarded $1,750,000 plus a new Winnebago.'

- 'January 2000: Kathleen Robertson of Austin, Texas was awarded $780,000.00 by a jury of her peers after breaking her ankle tripping over a toddler who was running amuck inside a furniture store. The owners of the store were understandably surprised at the verdict, considering the misbehaving tyke was Ms. Robertson's son.'

- 'June 1998: A 19-year-old, Carl Truman of Los Angeles, won $74,000.00 and medical expenses when his neighbor ran his hand over with a Honda Accord. Mr. Truman apparently didn't notice someone was at the wheel of the car whose hubcap he was trying to steal.'

- 'October 1998: A Terrence Dickson of Bristol, Pennsylvania was exiting a house he finished robbing by way of the garage. He was not able to get the garage door to go up because the automatic door opener was malfunctioning. He couldn't re-enter the house because the door connecting the house and garage locked when he pulled it shut. The family was on vacation, so Mr. Dickson found himself locked in the garage for eight days. He subsisted on a case of Pepsi he found, and a large bag of dry dog food. This upset Mr. Dickson, so he sued the homeowner's insurance claiming the situation caused him undue mental anguish. The jury agreed to the tune of half a million dollars and change.'

- 'October 1999: Jerry Williams of Little Rock, Arkansas was awarded $14,500.00 and medical expenses after being bitten on the buttocks by his next door neighbor's beagle. The beagle was on a chain in its owner's fenced-in yard, as was Jerry. The award was less than sought after because the jury felt the dog may have been provoked by Jerry, who, at the time, was shooting it repeatedly with a pellet gun.'

- 'May 2000: A Philadelphia restaurant was ordered to pay Amber Carson of Lancaster, Pennsylvania $113,500.00 after she slipped on a spilled soft drink and broke her coccyx. The beverage was on the floor because Ms. Carson threw it at her boyfriend 30 seconds earlier during an argument.'

- 'December 1997: Kara Walton of Claymont, Delaware successfully sued the owner of a night club in a neighboring city when she fell from the bathroom window to the floor and knocked out her two front teeth. This occurred while Ms. Walton was trying to sneak through the window in the ladies room to avoid paying the $3.50 cover charge. She was awarded $12,000 and dental expenses.'

And then there's this one:

- 'Hershey's Ordered To Pay Obese Americans $135 Billion. In one of the largest product-liability rulings in U.S. history, the Hershey Foods Corporation was ordered by a Pennsylvania jury Monday to pay $135 billion in restitution fees to 900,000 obese Americans who for years consumed the company's fattening snack foods.'

That is a myth and not a myth. It's a satire from the *Onion* from August 2000. But events have caught up, as certain innovative legal theories gather strength in America. Fat law is evolving very quickly, as advanced legal theories find cases to fit them. We'll have a look at the legal genius – the evil legal genius, according to tort reformers – Professor John Banzhaf later on.

Brockovich I

While we're on the subject of myths: *Erin Brockovich*.

What a terrific film that was. The screenplay had Julia Roberts playing a former beauty queen who talked her unqualified way into a legal firm. She discovered evidence of a cancer cluster caused by chromium-6 pollution, and a power company's cover-up. She organised a class action, defeated the hot-shot lawyers from the big city and won $330 million in damages for the suffering people of Hinkley.

American tort reformers (who are viscerally and professionally opposed to everything Ms Brockovich has done) have discovered their own heroine in Norma Zager, a reporter on a small-circulation freesheet in Beverly Hills whose reports have shown the Brockovich myth in a different light.

Here's one post-Hinkley chapter in Erin's career.

Erin met a young graduate of Beverly Hills High School who had two types of cancer. Beverly Hills is one of the few high schools that have their own oil wells (only in America!). Mrs Brockovich-Ellis, as she now is, took some air samples and revealed that the level of benzene was five times higher around the school than it was on the freeway, and that such levels produced Hodgkin's disease at 16 times the level it should be among Beverly Hills graduates. It was Hinkley all over again.

'When I have three hundred cancers staring me in the face and an oil-production facility underneath the school, it doesn't take a rocket scientist to figure out that the two fit together,' Mrs B-E told *People* magazine. At the same time, she told Associated Press that the school's cancer rate was 20–30 times the national average.

The media storm went round the country. Norma Zager attended a few of the public meetings and – though she was no rocket scientist either – quickly suspected the story wasn't quite that simple. Government regulators had done their tests and found no significant amounts of benzene in the air. Erin and her boss Masry (whom we remember in the form of

Albert Finney) wouldn't answer any questions on the discrepancy.

Eventually Norma got hold of the original research at the lab that Masry used to compile the data. This has a remarkable echo of the film, where Erin inveigles her way into the records office and finds the company has been suppressing incriminating facts.

Norma claims that Brockovich and Masry had done no epidemiological study and, of the 300 'cancer' cases, only 94 were actual formal diagnosis of cancer, with the others ranging from symptoms such as insomnia to 'tingling sensations'. Also, her own samples showed nearly all readings to be normal. The highest level was still below the state's regulated maximum.

'Oh, my God!' as they used to say in B-movies, 'I've become everything I've ever hated!' The compensation queen had learned too well from the corporates she had defeated.

Brockovich II

Let us return to the Hinkley case that made film history. That gets more complicated as time goes on. Some of the case doesn't seem to stand up to scientific enquiry. Kathleen Sharp wrote up her detailed critique into the case in the internet publication *Salon*.

Among the testimony she assembled was that of a toxicologist at the US Department of Health and Human

Services, who said that chromium-6 in water doesn't harm humans: 'It's very unlikely that people could die from drinking chromium-6 in the water, even over time.' Moreover, health studies found that the utility plant's own workers, who were likely exposed to at least as much pollution as neighbours were, had a life expectancy exceeding the California average.

So why did the PG&E – the big pollutant – pay up $333 million if the evidence against them was so poor? Well, the case was settled in private arbitration, so we don't know. This private justice system is a growing feature of American legal life. Amongst the criticism, there are suggestions that there was an appearance of friendship between the arbitrators and the lawyers. And finally, there was testimony that the power utility had broken the law by hiring detectives to snoop into the plaintiff lawyer's financial records.

That sort of behaviour is *really* punished at law (directors could go to jail for that).

But the $333 million created real bitterness in the community. Sharpe says, 'Many of the townspeople who sued complain their awards were smaller than they deserved. Some have even hired lawyers to get back excessive legal fees charged to children. Some claimants say that their lawyers kept their compensation awards for some months after the money was delivered, and that they didn't receive interest on it. They complain that there was little or no apparent logic behind the varying amounts of money individual plaintiffs received; some claim that the arbitrators never even looked at their medical records.

'One elderly resident "blew up at one of the attorneys, who didn't like his attitude," according to a fellow townsman, and "got a real bad deal," and was allotted in the end only $25,000. "Fairly or not," writes Sharp, "some residents complained that if you were buddies with Ed and Erin you got more money."

Of the $333 million paid by PG&E, the lawyers kept 40 per cent plus $10 million for expenses. The money was held by Masry for six months. Then, the 650 plaintiffs got very different sums allocated to them and remain puzzled as to how allocation was decided. The sum would have provided $300,000 each. But 81 were interviewed and it was shown they received an average of $152,000. Many residents only got $50,000 or $60,000. The precise allocation was kept confidential.

You, the Jury

'Even the severest critic of the "compensation culture" would probably accept that there are some kinds of careless conduct for which a victim should be entitled to damages. The problem lies in defining the frontier between conduct that may give rise to legal liability and conduct that will not. Every inch of the line has been the subject of fiercely contested litigation.'

Lord Bingham

In *The Gripes of Wrath* in 2005, it was reported that two men had served 37 years in jail for a crime they hadn't committed. On release they were given £350,000 compensation. But £62,000 had been deducted for board and lodging while they'd been in prison (it's an eighteenth-century idea that has survived, somehow). Injustice is a big feature of human life – it doesn't change.

But compensation is one of the few ways we can successfully bite back at personal injustices that have been done us. What if you've been beaten up by prison guards? Raped by a priest as a child? Poisoned by a defective product? Run down by a drunken driver? How about being told to go out onto unsafe scaffolding? Or sent out in a brakeless vehicle? Or made to work in a building with Legionnaires' disease in the air conditioning?

Why wouldn't you seek redress? If your child suffers an injury you can't explain adequately, social services (particularly in certain parts of the country) are very likely to take him or her away, along with all siblings, and forcibly adopt them out. There is no appeal, no redress and no compensation when the decision turns out to have been a vicious, vindictive act on the part of stupid and unpleasant social workers. Is that worth a million?

The powers that be are indeed remote from us, in many ways beyond our reach. Without the threat of a suit – and more particularly without the financial penalty they have to pay if they lose – they would run their services much more for their benefit than for ours.

Doctor? No!

Here's an anecdote from Michael Beverley, director of Claims4Free.co.uk. He is quoting Noel Ranger, a 24-year-old carer from Birmingham:

'The police said they were taking me down the station because I had no tax. I told them I'd only just picked up a new bike from the garage and hadn't got round to sorting out the tax. One of the officers asked me to put my arm out so he could handcuff me. I said there was no need because I'd go willingly. But they insisted and one of the officers pulled my arm right behind my back and twisted it. The pain was awful ... At the station I asked to see a doctor but they put me straight in a cell ... They later said that I was free to go and I wasn't charged with anything. I asked to see a police doctor again and they told me to wait at the front desk. I waited an hour but nobody turned up. In the end I called one of my brothers and he took me to the City Hospital.'

If you weren't allowed to pursue a private claim for compensation, what could you do? Go through the police complaints procedure? You might end up with an apology – which the officers concerned could email to you before going to the back of the shop to clang a prisoner's head in the cell doors.

Members of the jury ...

Try to imagine yourself sitting in on the jury in the following cases.

Takes your breath away

In Paddington Station, the drivers sometimes leave their train engines running. The station fills up with acrid diesel fumes. You complain but nothing happens. What if you sought damages on account of an asthmatic attack and they made sure that engines were turned off? Would that be fair enough? How about damages to prevent an asthmatic attack that you hadn't had? How about – because you aren't asthmatic at all – damages to prevent someone else suffering an asthmatic attack?

It's just potty!

Until recently a number of Scottish prisons provided inmates with chamber pots rather than in-cell toilets for overnight use. After a civil suit for compensation, the practice has now been ruled a human rights violation.

Spanky hanky-panky

A tribunal has awarded a woman almost £26,000 after her boss threatened to spank her.

Hayley Swanson's boss, Neil Riddell, accused her of hypersensitivity. On one occasion, Mr Riddell stood behind her when she was bending over to stack some team merchandise and said, 'Your bum wants a good spanking. It's smiling at me. I'm going to put you over my knee and spank you.' Mr Riddell said he was trying to boost her self-esteem through the 'additional attention'.

The tribunal held that Ms Swanson faced 'highly inappropriate behaviour' during her employment at the McLaren Formula One Team Fan Club and rejected Mr Riddell's defence.

Was that a good thing or a bad thing?

Blowing the whistle

Ian Perkin was the chief financial officer of St George's Hospital and in 2001 uncovered a systematic deception by which the hospital was fiddling the count of cancelled operations and thereby meeting government imposed targets.

At the disciplinary hearing (after which he was sacked), the case was heard by a woman who'd been trying to get rid of him for some time. For his 'disruptive personality'? Because he had called the chief executive (who later retired early on grounds of ill health) 'a liar' and 'a bully'? Or because he was revealing systematic deceptions?

Though he was not accused of any misconduct, he was sacked. An employment tribunal found that he had been unfairly dismissed because the disciplinary hearing had been chaired by someone who had arranged for him to be removed. But then the tribunal declared, surprisingly, that Mr Perkin had contributed 100 per cent towards his dismissal because he had attacked the integrity of his colleagues by revealing their systematic deception. Even if a different disciplinary procedure had been used, he said, Mr Perkin would not have been kept on.

Lord Chief Justice Wall said, 'Mr Perkin was, of course, entitled to defend himself, but the manner of his defence, and in particular his attacks on the honesty, financial probity and integrity of his colleagues ... opened the door in my judgment to the tribunal being able to find that any other disciplinary process would have ended with the same result.'

Going down ...

In the case of *Mr A* v. *Unnamed school* in May 2000, record compensation of £300,000 was awarded. Mr A, a teacher, was pushed down some stairs during a disciplinary disturbance at a school in Shropshire. While he was physically uninjured, he became irrational and started suffering from delusions and has been unable to work ever since.

It is a story that can make those of us who enjoy that sort of thing scrabble at our chests and bark at the night. There are some very potent words and phrases in there: unhurt; delusions; teacher; unable to work ever since; £300,000. That's a lot of money. You could buy a street of terraced houses in some parts of the country with that. And we've only Mr A's word for it that he's been mentally injured.

The longer report from the National Union of Teachers may be one-sided but it presents a boss-from-hell picture of a head teacher who presided over a culture of bullying, disrespect, foolishness and incompetence. It's impossible to know how true this is, as the unnamed head teacher would doubtless tell the story in different terms.*

How do you rule?

---

* There is one tell-tale remark in the plaintiff's evidence that casts doubt on the authenticity of his pitch for compensation: 'I was unable to distinguish my dreams, which were solely about work, from reality.' Oh, really? Did he really dream solely about work? As we know, that's the sort of thing you have to say in these cases.

Fire hazards

Here are two reports of the famous fireman's knee:

FIREMEN BANNED FROM GYM BECAUSE OF INVISIBLE DUST

Nigel Bunyan, *Daily Telegraph*

'Firemen have been banned from exercising for fear of falling victim to a new hazard: invisible dust. Tony McGuirk, Merseyside's chief fire officer, has told his employees that they must not use exercise machines or go circuit training in their stations. He imposed the ban after being sued by a fireman who slipped on unseen dust and tore ligaments in his knee. The Court of Appeal ordered Merseyside Fire Service to pay Gavin Bassie, 38, £100,000 compensation and a similar amount in legal costs.

'Yesterday Mr McGuirk expressed his exasperation at a "ridiculous" ruling that could affect crews throughout the country. "Its effect is that we now need to deal with the presence of invisible dust in locations which are used for physical activity," he said.

'Mr Bassie slipped while exercising with colleagues at Liverpool's Old Swan fire station. His Honour Judge Platt, sitting at Liverpool County Court, decided that the accident, which ended the fireman's career, had been caused by a layer of dust that could not be seen by the naked eye. The fire service took the case to the Court of Appeal but lost. Peter Rushton, a fire service spokesman, said: "We thought we had carried out all the risk assessments we could. But how do you assess a risk that can't be seen?"'

And here is the TUC report of the same affair.

'Gavin Bassie, a fire-fighter, suffered a catastrophic knee injury in a fall during a PT exercise on a dusty floor that ended his 13-year career. The press and the Merseyside Fire Authority have sought to present the case as compensation culture, when it is in fact anything but. The Fire Authority was in breach of the Health and Safety at Work regulations.

'Mr Bassie originally offered to settle his claim without recourse to lawyers, for £40,000. By refusing to admit liability and by defending Mr Bassie's claim all the way to the Court of Appeal, the Fire Authority has been landed with a £200,000 bill for damages and costs. The Court did not believe the Fire Brigade's witnesses, and criticised them heavily for the way in which they investigated the accident. However, the court did not suggest that anything onerous needed to be done to prevent further similar accidents. The floor simply had to be cleaned before PT exercises.'

The unions say the authority engaged in black propaganda, threatening to freeze recruitment and close down the PT programme; it was part of their industrial-relations strategy, no doubt. The other side would point out that a tough-guy firefighter wanted £40,000 for having slipped and torn ligaments in his knee. Why didn't the players themselves make sure the floor was clean? Is that beneath a fireman's dignity? It wasn't a 'catastrophic' injury for a fireman, as the union keeps pointing out. A 'catastrophic injury' for a fireman would be caused by a burning house falling on him.

You can get surgery to fix a torn ligament. You can get back to work. It's not the end of a career fighting fires. And what's wrong with a desk job? And the fire service says, 'Its effect is that we now need to deal with the presence of invisible dust in locations which are used for physical activity ... We thought we had carried out all the risk assessments we could. But how do you assess a risk that can't be seen?'

Who knows? There's always the possibility of sweeping the floor. It's a tightly fought case and our sympathies would swing both ways in the room, if we heard all the evidence. This is the way industrial relations are conducted in the court room now that unions carry less clout.

Ups and downs

Camilla's bodyguard made the headlines when he was appointed. It looks like he was presented to the media as the first black man promoted to that level. The job went wrong in ways we can't know, and he was moved. He sued, using a novel legal idea. He alleged he had been promoted only for reasons of 'political correctness' – because he was black – and that without proper training and support he was out of his depth and this led to his being sacked from his prestigious post. He shouldn't have been promoted in the first place, and he shouldn't have been demoted in the second. Thus: a year's pay on the nail by way of apology.

I rang up the Met's press office to see what the score was. 'Sergeant Leslie Turner,' I said, 'Camilla's bodyguard, £30,000 compensation for being over-promoted.'

The press officer called up the file on his screen and went through it. 'Mm hm, mm hm,' he went for about a minute, reading through. Then he must have come to a new screen because he said crisply, 'Right. We don't comment on that story.'

'What, at all?'

'Not at all.'

That probably means the story is true, or true enough. They've settled out of court and are embarrassed by everything about it. Normally a settlement includes a confidentiality clause so nothing can be released.

I have a sneaking regard for Sergeant Turner. If he was being used to meet targets (so that the minister could stand up in the Commons and congratulate himself on implementing successfully the government's ethnic-involvement strategy) – if he was being used for some ulterior purpose – then he deserves a little compensation. Mind you, I wouldn't mind a year's salary in compensation for being overpromoted.

But the fact that no one is prepared to talk about the award is further evidence that the level of compensation settlements and costs is probably impossible to ascertain.

There was a soldier ...

The mother of a Scottish soldier killed in Iraq had plans to sue the Ministry of Defence over her son's death. Rose Gentle believes the MoD was negligent and breached its duty of care by not equipping the patrol on which her 19-year-old son Gordon was serving with an electronic signal-jamming device that might have prevented a roadside bombing in Basra in June 2004, in which the younger Gordon lost his life.

Is that a good suit or a bad suit? Remember all the assurances that the minister and the ministry made before the Iraq war, that every soldier was fully equipped? We then found out that they didn't have desert boots. That the tanks lacked filters to keep out chemicals and gas. That the troops didn't have enough guns. That they were sharing ammunition.

Why not sue? Even punitively?

The reason a lot of the kit didn't arrive in time for the war against Saddam was political. No preparations were allowed until the decision to invade had been finalised. The PM couldn't allow the perception that he'd already made up his mind to invade while the UN was still debating the matter. So the army had a very few weeks to get its logistics together prior to D-Day.

The troops went in — for the worst possible reasons — by the seat of their pants.

If the claim succeeds and Mrs Gentle gets a big payout, maybe the powers that be will think twice about that next time.

Without reference

In 2000, one Belinda Coote, the former manager of a bowling alley, got £195,000 after her employer refused to supply a letter of reference.

She had won a sex-discrimination case against her employers (Granada Hospitality) in 1993. Over the following two years, she tried to get work through two employment agencies but her prospects were 'crucified' by Granada's refusal to supply a reference. In 1995, an employment tribunal turned down her case. Ms Coote (who is now a magistrate, incidentally) took the case to the European Court of Justice, who ruled in her favour, and the English tribunal accepted the judgment and compensation was agreed with Granada.

Put like that, it sounds reasonable. But, then again, we swing to and fro as counsel put other arguments to us ...

Adjusted for inflation, the award was the best part of a quarter of a million pounds. Five or six years' pay, say. Were Ms Coote's job prospects really 'crucified'? Is it really impossible to get a job without references any more? Are we back to Victorian times when to be dismissed without references was to be condemned to paupery?

Warning: eating can damage your health

A very, very fat person asks for a Big Mac – should we let them have it? At what point will counter staff be legally liable for handing out obviously damaging food? 'I think you've had enough, sir'? Shouldn't soft drinks carry a warning? The Government Dentist recommends brushing after drinking? This drink will make you fat and can cause heart disease and diabetes?

The logic that will drive these absurdities will come down to the level of tax and public healthcare. It goes like this: 'The fact that self-inflicted fat damages a person is of no concern to me, unless I have to pay for it. If I am liable for their healthcare, then I have a direct interest in that person's self-control and calorie intake. If I'm paying for the consequences, I have the right to ask McDonald's staff to refuse service to these people. And the government (who will administer the subsequent healthcare) has a duty to do all it can to prevent self-inflicted harm in order to focus care and public money on other more innocent people who haven't inflicted damage on themselves.'

Once this argument gets into the public domain (I give it another generation), there will be less and less tolerance for the abnormal. To be decent we will have to be normal. 'Deviations from the mean cause innocent children to die!'

If you happen to find that proposition unlikely, it will get easier as the years go by.

A lot of bottle

Here is a case from July 2003. A Brighton couple consisting of a property tycoon and a heroin-addicted escort girl had a heated argument on holiday in Barbados. Nicola Richardson alleged that her partner assaulted her with a bottle, causing bruises, and lacerations to her scalp and hand. The couple were deported and they broke up shortly thereafter. Ian Howie was later convicted of trying to hire a gunman to murder Nicola Richardson, and was sent to jail for six years. Ms Richardson then sued him for damages and aggravated damages and damages for the gifts he'd given, and taken back, during their three-year relationship.

She got £15,000 damages, and he appealed. The aggravated damages of £5,000 for hurt feelings, humiliation and so forth were reduced to £4,500.

Tribunal chairman Alistair McArthur ruled, 'Where a male person enters a ladies' toilet in the circumstances as the claimant described, that is in our view plainly an act of sex discrimination,' but rejected her other complaints. The tribunal ordered Kettle Produce to pay Mrs Ward, of Methil, £1,750 compensation for sex discrimination for injury to her feelings.

A tragic loss

Barry Welch, thought to be one of the youngest people in the UK to contract asbestos-related cancer, died on 27 April 2005. The 32-year-old father of three from Leicester was diagnosed with mesothelioma in 2004.

His family believe he was exposed to asbestos fibres as a child in the 1970s when his stepfather Roger Bugby worked for Palmers Scaffolding. It is thought the exposure came from contamination on Mr Bugby's clothing when he worked as a scaffolder on Kingsnorth Power Station, adjacent to the Isle of Grain. Mr Welch was diagnosed with the cancer in September 2004 and given just six months to live.

At the time, he said, 'I am an innocent victim. It just seems so unfair that my life will be cut short, even though I never knowingly came into contact or worked with asbestos.' Solicitors for the Welches are pursuing a claim for compensation against Mr Bugby's former employer.

Mr Welch was not eligible for industrial injuries benefit because his exposure to asbestos was not while working. And his family will have difficulty securing common-law compensation because they will have to deal with all the normal barriers to a successful compensation claim and will not only have to prove his stepfather was negligently exposed to asbestos, but that Mr Welch's exposure was also a result of the company's negligence. Can you help? The Welch family's solicitors, Irwin Mitchell, want to hear from anyone who worked with Roger Bugby for Palmers Scaffolding in the 1970s, or with a knowledge of working conditions on the Kingsnorth Power Station.

This case went through the House of Lords in 2006. What's your verdict?

Fat chance!

Over in America, a press release from the famous John Banzhaf, litigator extraordinary. He is hoping to do to fast-food companies what was done to tobacco companies. I scoff, naturally, but once the logic starts gripping you, it's hard to avoid getting sucked in. (*Don't look into his eyes!*)

'The sixth fat law suit has just been successful, with McDonald's paying $8.5 million to settle it in addition to its agreement to pay $12.5 million to settle an earlier fat law suit. A third fat law suit, accusing the company of contributing to the obesity of minors, was recently reinstated by a unanimous U.S. Court of Appeals.

'This brings to six the number of successful fat law suits which have so far been brought, and more are on the way. McDonald's and others initially labeled them frivolous, but the fast food giant obviously thinks they are serious enough to pay out over $20 million in the past several years to avoid damaging jury verdicts.

'The first successful fat law suit against McDonald's was put together by Prof. Banzhaf's law students, and charged McDonald's with failing to disclose that its

French fries contained beef fat. McDonald's settled it by paying $12.5 million, and making the required disclosure. The fat law suit settled today charged McDonald's with failing to inform consumers of delays in a plan to reduce fat in the cooking oil used for its popular French fries and other foods. It will now pay to make those disclosures, and to educate the public about the deadly dangers of trans fat in foods.

'Two earlier fat law suits against food companies for failing to properly disclose the fat and calorie content of their products were settled for a combined total of about $8 million. Another suit forced Kraft Foods to take the trans fat out of its Oreo cookies, thereby substantially reducing the risk and the calories. Another law suit was the catalyst that forced New York City to ban sugary soft drinks and most fattening foods from its schools.

'Even just the threat of a law suit forced the Seattle School Board to back down on plans to renew a "Coke For Kickbacks" contract under which students would have been able to buy sugary soft drinks during the school day with the school getting a share of the profits, and four federal judges have all now held that the legal theories under which children seek to hold McDonald's liable for its fair share of causing them to become obese are meritorious.

'Be assured that more fat suits are on the way, and that this most recent victory will encourage other lawyers concerned about obesity to consider joining this growing movement. It took more than thirty years after the Surgeon General's report on smoking for plaintiffs to win any money, yet six fat law suits have now been successful within only a few years of the Surgeon General's December 2001 report on obesity.'

Banzhaf says that a co-ordinated number of law suits are likely to be filed in several different states. All are aimed at protecting children, as was the lawsuit against McDonald's recently reinstated by the US Court of Appeals for the 2d Circuit.

US Mania

The Michigan Lawsuit Abuse organisation runs a 'Wacky Warnings' competition every year. Manufacturers hear about the wilder compensation cases and (whether or not the cases are true) decide to put warnings on their products 'just in case'. Frankly, some of them are so preposterous you assume they're made up. But, at http://www.mlaw.org/wwl/index.html, they provide photographs of the labels.

Since 1997, the past winners of the Michigan Lawsuit Abuse have been the following.

WARNING LABELS

A label on a kitchen knife warns: **'Never try to catch a falling knife.'**

A cocktail napkin has a map of the waterways around Hilton Head, South Carolina printed on it, along with this: **'Caution: Not to be used for navigation.'**

A warning label on a bottle of dried bobcat urine, made to keep rodents and other pests away from garden plants, says, **'Not for human consumption.'**

A warning label on a baking pan: **'Ovenware will get hot when used in oven.'**

A label on a baby stroller warns, **'Remove child before folding.'**

A brass fishing lure with a three-pronged hook on the end warns, **'Harmful if swallowed.'**

A popular scooter for children warns, **'This product moves when used.'**

A nine-by-three-inch bag of air used as packing material cautions, **'Do not use this product as a toy, pillow, or flotation device.'**

A flushable toilet brush warns, **'Do not use for personal hygiene.'**

The label on an electric hand blender promoted for use in 'blending, whipping, chopping and dicing' warns, **'Never remove food or other items from the blades while the product is operating.'**

A digital thermometer that can be used to take a person's temperature several different ways warns, **'Once used rectally, the thermometer should not be used orally.'**

A household iron warns users, **'Never iron clothes while they are being worn.'**

A label on a hairdryer reads, **'Never use hair dryer while sleeping.'**

A warning on an electric drill made for carpenters cautions, **'This product is not intended for use as a dental drill.'**

The label on a bottle of drain cleaner warns, **'If you do not understand, or cannot read, all directions, cautions and warnings, do not use this product.'**

A smoke detector warns, **'Do not use the Silence Feature in emergency situations. It will not extinguish a fire.'**

A massage chair warns, **'DO NOT use massage chair without clothing ... '** and, **'Never force any body part into the backrest area while the rollers are moving.'**

A cardboard car sunshield that keeps sun off the dashboard warns, **'Do not drive with sunshield in place.'**

An 'Aim-n-Flame' fireplace lighter cautions, **'Do not use near fire, flame or sparks.'**

A label on a hand-held massager advises consumers not to use **'while sleeping or unconscious'**.

A 12-inch rack for storing compact discs warns, **'Do not use as a ladder.'**

A cartridge for a laser printer warns, **'Do not eat toner.'**

A 13-inch wheel on a wheelbarrow warns, **'Not intended for highway use.'**

A can of self-defence pepper spray warns users, **'May irritate eyes.'**

A warning on a pair of shin guards manufactured for cyclists says, **'Shin pads cannot protect any part of the body they do not cover.'**

A snow-clearing machine warns: **'Do not use snowthrower on roof.'**

A dishwasher carries this warning: **'Do not allow children to play in the dishwasher.'**

A popular manufactured fireplace log warns, **'Caution – Risk of Fire.'**

A box of birthday cake candles says, **'DO NOT use soft wax as ear plugs or for any other function that involves insertion into a body cavity.'**

Heavy going

A number of children in New York were killed by TV sets falling on them. The deaths have prompted a plea by some grieving mothers for new laws that would insist on warning labels about the potential danger of top-heavy or poorly placed TVs.

'If there were warning labels, or if there was any awareness that this could be a danger, believe me, the kind of mother I am, I wouldn't have even let my son have a TV in his room,' Michele DeMeo-Bonsangue told the *New York Post* in 2006.

Warning: This television is subject to the law of gravity!

Warning: Sitting too close to the television will not damage your eyes. However, if it falls on you, it will kill you!

⁓

US lawyers earn $50 billion in legal fees per year, with a significant portion coming from their percentage of lawsuit winnings.

The legal excesses of America will not happen in Britain. Juries don't decide awards for personal injuries (judges do). And the loser-pays principle discourages the more frivolous suits. Also, in America, you can shop around for the jurisdiction best suited to your case (there are wide and wild variations in the standards in different states).

Many of the best cases get turned down, but they go on for years until they reach that point, and they prompt other cases as their lives go on.

⁓

Grace Fuller claimed that she suffered two epileptic seizures because a flight attendant used the phrase 'Eenie, meenie, minie, mo, pick a seat, we gotta go' to passengers boarding an open-seating flight late. Ms Fuller and her travelling companion, both African-Americans, ascribed racist meaning to the phrase and sued under a variety of federal and state claims. It is a novel medical theory that racism causes epileptic episodes. Too novel for any of the courts. The claims failed.

Three little birds ...

The winner of the 2002 True Stella Awards (awards for the most perverse and annoying lawsuits of the year) ... Sisters Janice Bird, Dayle Bird Edgmon and Kim Bird Moran sued their mother's doctors and the hospital in which she received treatment. Janice had accompanied her mother to a minor medical procedure. When something went wrong, Janice and Dayle witnessed doctors rushing their mother to emergency surgery. Rather than malpractice, their legal fight centred on the 'negligent infliction of emotional distress'. It wasn't the distress caused to their mother, but the distress caused to them when they saw doctors rushing to help their mother. The case was fought all the way to the California Supreme Court, which finally ruled against the women.

And that's not entirely exceptional. There are cases of people suing for the stress of the possibility of contracting cancer, even when they are perfectly healthy. There have also been claims for the stress of seeing former colleagues suffering from asbestos-related disease. And we can't act superior in that, since our Hillsborough police officers got more than the Hillsborough victims (see Chapter 3).

Richard N. Shick, while employed as a caseworker in the Illinois Department of Public Aid, robbed a convenience store in Joliet, Illinois, armed with a sawn-off shotgun. Afterwards, he sued the department, claiming that he was discriminated against because of his disabilities and his sex, the trauma of which caused him to commit the robbery.

The jury awarded him $5 million in damages and $166,700 in back pay. The US District Court for the Southern District of Illinois partially vacated and dismissed the judgment, but awarded $303,830 in front pay, even while he served a ten-year sentence.

Shot in the foot

A drug-enforcement agent, Lee Paige, picked up an 'unloaded' gun during a safety demonstration and pulled the trigger. He told the roomful of school-children, 'I am the only person in this room professional enough to handle this gun!' He pulled the trigger again and shot himself in the foot.

The videotape of the demonstration found its way onto the Internet and the agent sued because he 'became and is the target of jokes, derision, ridicule and disparaging comments. Mr Paige has also been subjected to such comments made to his wife and children. Mr Paige has been frequently confronted with embarrassing and humiliating comments from people both inside and outside the United States about the accidental discharge, including interalia, by people at restaurants, grocery stores and airports. White supremacy organizations have used the videotape to ridicule black Americans in general and Mr Paige in particular. Because he became highly recognizable as a result of the disclosure of the videotape, Mr Paige has been unable to act as an undercover agent. As a result of the notoriety arising from the disclosure of the videotape, Mr Paige is no longer permitted or able to give educational motivational speeches and presentation.'

Note: He is suing because he is no longer able to give safety presentations. And he is no longer able to give these presentations because people know he let off a loaded gun in front of a room of children, causing actual bodily harm.

∿

The mother of a Granville, Illinois man, who shot himself in 2005 at the Spring Valley Jail, has filed a wrongful-death suit against the city, the police chief and a former police officer. Robert McFadin, placed in a holding cell after being charged with violating an order of protection against his estranged wife, wrested away the gun of former Spring Valley police officer Thomas Quartucci and beat him up.

When Quartucci fled the cell, McFadin used the gun to shoot himself. Quartucci, who was admitted to intensive care after the beating and remained on workers' compensation until retirement, is among the defendants in the suit. It is alleged that the officer violated procedure when he did not secure his loaded weapon before entering the cell.

⁓

Father David Hanser, aged 70, was one of the first Catholic priests to be caught up in the sex-abuse scandal. In 1990, he settled a suit filed by one of his victims for $65,000. In the settlement, the priest agreed not to work with children any more, but the victim later learned that he was ignoring that part of the agreement. The victim appealed to the Church, asking it to stop Hanser from working near children, but the Church wouldn't intervene.

When the outraged victim went to the Press to warn the public that a paedophile priest was working near children, Hanser sued him for his $65,000 in return because the victim violated his part of the deal – to keep the settlement secret.

Bog standard

In March 1995, a San Diego man unsuccessfully attempted to sue the city and its Jack Murphy Stadium, which is the home to major-league football and baseball teams. Robert Glaser claimed the stadium's unisex toilet policy caused him emotional distress, thanks to the sight of a woman using a urinal in front of him.

Mr Glaser subsequently tried 'six or seven' other toilets in the stadium, only to find women in all of them. He asserted he 'had to hold it in for four hours' because he was too embarrassed to share the public toilets with women. He asked for $5.4 million. He didn't get it.

A San Carlos, California man sued the Escondido Public Library for $1.5 million. His dog, a 50-pound Labrador cross, was attacked in November 2000 by the library's 12-pound feline mascot, LC (also known as Library Cat). He lost.

Bumming around

In 1994, a student at the University of Idaho unsuccessfully sued that institution over his fall from a third-floor dorm window. He'd been showing his butt to other students when the window gave way. It was contended the university failed to provide a safe environment for students or to properly warn them of the dangers inherent in revealing your lower parts from upper-storey windows.

McDonald's found itself in another drink-related suit. A man who had placed a milkshake between his legs, leaned over, while driving, to reach into his bag of food and squeezed the milkshake container in the process.

When the lid popped off and spilled half the drink in his lap, the driver became distracted and ran into another man's car. That man in turn tried to sue McDonald's for causing the accident, saying the restaurant should have cautioned the man who had hit him against eating while driving. He didn't get anything.

~

Marissa Imrie was just 14 when she caught a cab and rode 50 miles to San Francisco's Golden Gate Bridge. She jumped off, killing herself. Her mother sued the bridge authority, complaining it should have built an 'effective' suicide barrier because the bridge is well known as the world's most popular suicide spot. Stretching credulity, the suit claimed that the lack of such a barrier was a violation of the girl's constitutional right to life. As if that wasn't enough, the suit argued the mother's rights were also violated: her 'Constitutional right of familial association'.

~

'The plaintiffs have presented some evidence that 17-year-old males generally do not have fully mature brains, and as such cannot fully control their impulses or appreciate some risks,' District Judge Lawrence Stengel wrote, allowing the idea that an 'attractive nuisance' (in this case, 12,000-volt train-powering wires) can attract not just infants but 17-year-olds.

Police in South Carolina received a report of a vehicle trying to run down a pedestrian. When officers arrived, the suspect vehicle sped away and they gave chase. In his attempts to elude the officers, Ron Brown, 23, drove into a marked road-construction area and drove off the end of an unfinished bridge.

Mr Brown's father sued for wrongful death, naming not only the city and its police department, but also the construction company, the state department of transportation, the apartment complex where the chase started and the person who called the police to report the attempted murder.

She got the bug

Leslie Fox stayed in a hotel in the Catskills in 2005 for five nights and suffered, she said, 500 bites from bedbugs. She experienced 'great mental and physical pain'. The hotel offered her two free nights with them. She declined their offer and sued for $20 million in 2006. Confusingly, she went back to the same hotel and stayed in the same part of it with her husband two weeks after the $20 million incident.

A six-year-old boy was suspended from his school's first grade for three days for 'sexual harassment' because he allegedly put 'two fingers inside [a] girl's waistband while she sat on the floor in front of him', according to an Associated Press story.

∾

Two secretaries sued school official Thomas J. Kirschling for a comment he made in July 2002: 'I ride them hard and put them away wet.'

They sent him a memo saying they were outraged. He later explained it was a rural idiom that means someone is tired or worked hard. The saying is taken from the need to cool down a horse after strenuous exercise. Only a mistreated horse is stabled while it is still sweating. He apologised.

The two secretaries wanted $25,000 – and got it. The school board approved the settlement, although some members considered the amount excessive. Board member John Devlin said, 'It's nuts, though.'

∾

Wal-Mart Stores, the largest food chain in the United States, said in 2006 that it would no longer donate nearly expired or expired food to local groups feeding the hungry. A spokesman said the policy was an attempt to protect the corporation from liability in case someone who ate the donated food became sick.

I should point out that in my own household, refrigerated (but unfrozen) food a month past its sell-by date is regarded as fit for consumption. Experience tells me this is the case. Sell-by dates are very, very precautionary. The idea of throwing food away because it's a few hours rather than a few months past its date is incomprehensible to me. My children are more modern. They have no difficulty understanding the case. They won't eat food past its sell-by date. I once gave them an omelette at Easter made with eggs bought before Christmas (you could tell the eggs were fine). The boys felt ill only when I came clean two days later (the mind is powerful).

~

A drunken man – Juan Alejandro Soto – jumped onto the railway tracks and tried to outrun a train. He failed – and lost. He sued because the train operator didn't stop in time. He won $1.4 million.

Legal Exhibitionists

A federal government employee in Canada set out to sue Air Canada for more than $500,000 because he could not order a 7-Up in French. Michel Thibodeau won a favourable determination from the Commissioner of Official Languages over the incident on an internal flight. Mr Thibodeau, who is fluently bilingual, wanted $525,000 and an apology.

As it is extremely hard not to understand the words '7-Up' in any Indo-European language, one senses some political purpose behind the altercation. Many such extravagant cases are brought to court by legal exhibitionists in the States. They know that a multi-million dollar headline will bring valuable publicity.

In the same spirit, a Massachusetts mother sued a television for company for broadcasting advertisements for junk cereal breakfasts. She demanded £1.2 billion. Billion, that is. This isn't a search for justice or redress. This is social activism.

Smart Ass

In 1997, Bob Craft, of Hot Springs, Montana, legally changed his name to 'Jack Ass'. He was promoting an ass-based campaign for road safety. After the TV show and movie *Jackass* (theme song: 'If you're gonna be dumb, ya gotta be tough') generated huge profits, Mr Ass claimed the show's idea was plagiarised from him, infringed his trademarks and copyrights and demeaned, denigrated and damaged his public image. No attorney would take the case, so he filed suit on his own against the producers, demanding $50 million in damages. He was living in his car at the time. He lost his case. Later he shot himself in the head.

Don't cry for me ...

In Argentina, Dr Carlos Traboulsi, president of the local Christian Democrats, filed a $67 billion claim against Britain in a local court, citing the unlawful occupation/exploitation of the Falklands/Malvinas islands since 1833, as well as 'the theft of the River Plate Viceroy treasury in 1806'.

'We're seeking $67 billion compensation on behalf of the Argentine people because of the illegal and illegitimate use, usufruct [right to use another's property] and exploitation by Great Britain of the archipelago since 1833, and the theft of the Viceroy treasury in 1806,' Dr Traboulsi explained.

He also said it was 'mere coincidence' that the claim was made just 24 hours before Argentina had to repay the International Monetary Fund $3.1 billion.

'We've worked for five years on this demand and it is a complete coincidence that it should come to light as a tool to show the world that Argentines are not only debtors of an illegitimate debt but creditors of the foreign powers that robbed and looted the country,' he said.

~

Ten plaintiffs are suing Lloyd's of London in New York, demanding that it pay reparations for having written insurance on slave ships hundreds of years ago.

A colonial expedition to subjugate an African kingdom in the nineteenth century could bankrupt Britain if a Ugandan king succeeds in his £3.7 trillion (that's trillion, not billion) suit against the Crown. During a five-year war in the 1890s the British deposed King Kabalega II of the Bunyoro kingdom. His descendant, named King Solomon, has now retained lawyers in both Uganda and London and plans a legal action in the latter city. The money sought is equivalent to nearly a decade of British government public spending.

It's a smoke scream

American tort law had always operated on the principle of 'no harm, no foul'. This has changed. Without claiming any smoking-related harm, plaintiffs in one class action against tobacco companies were awarded $10.1 billion. They claimed to be the victims of deceptive advertising of 'light' and 'low-tar' cigarettes, despite the companies' warnings and compliance with strict federal guidelines.

Author Michael S. Greve asks in *Harm-Less Lawsuits? What's Wrong with Consumer Class Actions*, 'Should a plaintiff have to prove that he or she was harmed by the defendant's product when suing for damages? Lawsuits against pharmaceutical, electronic, tobacco, and fast-food companies have been allowed to proceed under broadly worded state laws against fraud, misleading advertising, and general unfair business dealing, and have eliminated the need to prove injury. The result is billion-dollar verdicts and settlements for consumer classes whose harms are purely hypothetical.'

A coalition of lawyers who have actively and successfully sued tobacco companies say they're close to filing a class-action lawsuit against soft-drink makers for selling sugared pop in schools. The lawyers have been trying to develop a case against the soft-drink makers for more than two years.

Lead counsel Richard Daynard said that, while the legal theory is ready, the challenge is finding the right set of parents to sign on as plaintiffs for the class-action case. 'It's taking us longer than we expected,' he said.

Eric Berlin (a US tort-reform advocate) remarks, 'So they don't actually have any angry parents or obese children begging for justice. All they have is a legal theory, a plaintiff-friendly state and a strong desire to sap billions from a juicy target. You know, I think with a case like this, trial lawyers might start to get something of a bad reputation.'

16

Is the Tide on the Turn?

The drift isn't all one way. The culture responds to rulings from the High Court, the Court of Appeal and the House of Lords. But the fame of undeserving cases gets very wide publicity, prompting other, similar cases to be brought, while adverse judgments attract much less publicity (there's so little indignation involved).

Jean Gratton was lying on the beach during her package holiday in the Caribbean when a coconut fell on her chest. 'It could have been fatal,' she said, suing Airtours, the tour operators on the other side of the world, who had sold her the package. She got £1,700. Travel operators became so worried about compensation claims, it was said at the time, that they established a £1 billion fighting fund to contest cases and make pay-outs. That was in 1999.

She wouldn't get that money now. The law changed. Travel companies can no longer be sued for events on the other side of the world.

In *Barrett* v. *Ministry of Defence* in 1995, a naval airman died of drunkenness. His widow sued the MoD for their failure to prevent naval drunkenness and to prevent her husband's death. The Court of Appeal held that only the deceased was responsible for his own drunkenness and it was neither reasonable nor justified to blame one adult for another's lack of control.

In *Mulcahy* v. *Ministry of Defence* in 1996, a soldier serving in the Gulf War suffered damage to his hearing when a fellow soldier fired a shell from a howitzer. It was held that no 'duty of care in negligence' existed between two active soldiers. Nor was there a duty on the Ministry of Defence to maintain a safe system of work in battle situations. The Court of Appeal found that there was no basis upon which the scope of the duty of care could be extended to such situations. Although the elements of proximity and foreseeability of damage were present, it was necessary to ask whether it was fair, just and reasonable to impose a duty of care in battle situations.

John Tomlinson suffered severe injuries by making a shallow dive into a lake at Brereton Heath Country Park in Cheshire. He became a tetraplegic and claimed substantial damages from the local council. The House of Lords eventually found in favour of the council. Their Lordships found that, although it had a duty of care to both visitors and trespassers to its property, it was not, on the facts of the case, reasonable to expect the council to protect Mr Tomlinson from his own actions.

'An important issue of freedom [was] at stake,' said Lord Hoffman. Lord Hobhouse said, 'It is not, and should never be, the policy of the law to require the protection of the foolhardy or reckless few to deprive, or interfere with, the enjoyment by the remainder of society of the liberties and amenities to which they are rightly entitled.'

Lord Scott added, 'Simply sporting about in the water with his friends, giving free rein to his exuberance. And why not? And why should the council be discouraged by the law of tort from providing facilities for young men and young women to enjoy themselves in this way? Of course there is some risk of accidents arising out of the *joie de vivre* of the young. But that is no reason for imposing a grey and dull safety regime on everyone.'

This judgment doesn't seem to have deterred local and low-level health and safety officials from busying themselves with more and more safety initiatives around open water.

What you gain on the swings ...

In 2004, *Simonds* v. *Isle of Wight* heard that a five-year-old child fell off a school swing and broke his arm. His mother sued the school, saying that the playground should have been taped off out of playtime hours. The court found that the council was not liable for the damage on the grounds that essentially a swing is a swing and does present an inherent and obvious risk. If a parent lets a child use a swing, the child might get hurt.

Nonetheless, playgrounds continue to get duller. The official play equipment of our day consists of a plastic cube with holes in it. Swings, roundabouts and vertiginous slides are, increasingly, period pieces.

In 2002, the Court of Appeal found against two teachers and a glass blower, two of whom were seeking six-figure sums for their "work-related depression". The judge found that one of them had problems at home which contributed to the ailment, and the other two hadn't made their employers aware of the problems.

Lady Justice Hale repudiated the idea that some jobs are of themselves more dangerous to mental health than others and ruled that 'occupational stress' was not the same as 'psychiatric injury'.

In July 2004, the House of Lords overturned Dunnachie (a legal decision that allowed hurt feelings to be compensated) and held that damages for injury to feelings are not recoverable in unfair-dismissal claims. Claims for hurt feelings in various forms still succeed, however, especially in sex-discrimination cases.

~

In June 2005, a judge rejected Margaret McTear's attempt to sue Imperial Tobacco over the death of her husband Alf. Lord Nimmo Smith, at the Court of Session in Edinburgh, said the test case failed on every count. He ruled that Mr McTear knew what he was doing and there was no proof that his cancer was caused by a particular cigarette brand.

Richard Daynard, a legal activist in America, called the ruling 'an extraordinarily ignorant opinion ... The UK suffers from a conservative, narrow-minded judiciary who don't know or don't want to know the relevant medical and social facts,' he said.

~

In 2006, the Law Lords ruled that lesser courts correctly threw out an application by passengers or their families seeking to sue two airlines, British Airways and China Airlines, for death and injury from deep-vein thrombosis (DVT). The action was a test case that could have thrown the air industry open to compensation claims for millions of pounds.

'There has seemingly been no media coverage at all for the English High Court's rejection of a claim brought by 36 people, mainly children, injured by hot drinks in McDonald's restaurants,' says barrister Richard Colbey, writing in the *Guardian*. 'Typical was nine-month-old Lamar Bentley, whose mother's coffee spilt on him in a Nottingham McDonald's when another customer accidentally knocked her tray. He required skin grafts under general anaesthetic.'

In June 2003, a High Court judge laid into the Health and Safety Executive (HSE) for wasting time and public money prosecuting the Metropolitan Police commissioner for failing to warn officers about the danger of climbing on roofs (one police officer died and another was injured after falling through roofs while on duty). Costs were estimated at £1 million in lawyers' fees and a further £2 million in investigations.

Had the HSE succeeded, the Met had planned to instruct its officers not to climb above head height. 'It would have been a veritable burglars' charter, a victory for criminals and would have encouraged suspects to use roofs to escape,' said one senior officer.

Ged away with yer!

In a landmark case in May 2005, 43-year-old Sandra Stevenson of Cawthorne Close in Kirkby, who made a false claim against Knowsley Metropolitan Borough Council, was prosecuted for her claim that she had tripped over a missing drain cover and shattered a disc in her back.

After considering the facts, the council and its insurers, Zurich Municipal, became suspicious of the claim. First, there had been three other claims from the same location in the city (word gets around the neighbourhood). Secondly, the type of injury the lady claimed to have sustained is not usually associated with an accident of that sort.

Once the official hospital records had been obtained, it was discovered that she had encountered the injury by, in her own words, 'pulling out bed'. When questioned in court the lady claimed – as inventively as you would expect from that part of the world – that she had said 'ged'. This was a dialect word, from her northeast heritage, that she claimed meant 'grid', and not 'bed'. She alleged that the hospital doctor had misheard her. They called in an expert in the Newcastle dialect, who testified that he had never heard or seen the word 'ged' before.

She was found guilty of attempted deception and sentenced to four months' imprisonment.

A part of the draft fifth EU Motor Insurance Directive proposed that compensation should be paid for personal injuries suffered by pedestrians and cyclists in accidents involving a motor vehicle, irrespective of whether the driver was at fault. This was struck out at a late stage, but it was a close thing. The idea is bubbling under, and maybe they'll have another go next time round.

Conclusion

There we were in the Savoy, 250 international ladies and me, sole male due to give an after-lunch entertainment. I had a thumping headache and sat out for a while to write the gay and witty speech they wanted (failing, rather, in the end). A Savoy employee asked if there was anything he could do. I asked for an aspirin. He could do anything except an aspirin. He wasn't allowed to give me an aspirin, or any medication. It was against company policy. In case anything went wrong. The Savoy would be liable for administering aspirin without medical authority.

The young man could *see* my head throbbing, and standing there for over a minute he could feel my headache start up in his own head. So he did everything he could. He went out and bought some aspirin himself and handed them to the organiser of the event who placed them on the table beside me. In order to avoid the possibility of litigation, should something have gone wrong.

What in the name of our sweet, suffering saviour have we come to?

The causes of this culture are elusive. There's no law that's made it happen. And they can't seem to pass a law to make it go away (they tried in 2006).

Our ordinary, civic lives have been interrupted in an extraordinary way by the law, by insurance companies, by health and safety officials, by experts, by an absurd and counterproductive reliance on qualifications. Compensation is the mechanism that gives real-life effect to these various influences. The cost of infringing modern safety rules is astonishing: of course people have become wary.

~

Just to try to take the politics out of this proposition for a minute.

There's nothing wrong with compensation per se. When wrongs are inflicted we need redress. There is no danger of Britain's compensation culture developing to the scale of the United States' (we have a 'loser-pays' rule in court cases, and, generally, juries aren't involved in awarding damages).

It may also be true that claims have fallen from their historic high, and maybe many people don't claim for everything they could do. Granted. All this may be the case. But, nonetheless, a culture of compensation has grown in the last generation; it is firmly rooted now and may grow or retreat but it isn't going to disappear. Compensation is a powerful weapon available to the individual in his or her struggle against an overmighty administration, but we also have the right and responsibility to try to mitigate its downside.

In that light, consider these propositions:

- It's very odd that people who can't pursue their chosen career through an accident can claim a right to a full salary in lieu, in perpetuity. If a policeman can't walk a beat because he's hurt his back, why wouldn't he be given a desk job instead of a full-salary pension for the rest of his life? If my career as a humorist was cut short by the death of my wife, would I be entitled to retire on an income-replacement policy for the next 40 years? Surely life is more uncertain than that.

- Highly paid traders and bankers are getting enormous pay-outs on sex-discrimination claims (sometimes for 'hurt feelings') because they are currently earning vast salaries and bonuses. Meanwhile, a nursery school teacher gets mutilated while defending her charges from a machete-wielding maniac – and she gets under £100,000. Is this just, or fair?

- When you add in the costs of faked, forged and phoney applications for incapacity benefit, early retirement, malingering on sick notes, and the time taken by teachers, doctors and emergency service personnel to defend claims that never go anywhere, the costs of a compensation culture are very much higher than any previous estimates. They run to tens of billions of pounds. If you add the direct costs to the loss of wages and the tax revenue foregone you get up to £50 billion without difficulty.

- Shouldn't self-diagnosed ailments be treated more cautiously in these depraved times? 'And I considered suicide' is a phrase that should not be allowed in court. Anyone can say it. Anyone can think it. Anyone can consider suicide for reasons other than 'stress at work'. If there is a fat pay-out dependent on 'considering suicide' then people will consider it — and very likely make their claim as realistic and plausible as possible (it's a dangerous road to start down). If you pay people for being depressed, it will create depression.

- The rate of recovery from accidents is very bad in this country. Paraplegics in Scandinavia get back to work after their trauma far more quickly and in far greater numbers than they do in Britain. The waste of human life this represents is a scandal. Daring research shows that the more compensation is paid, the worse this problem is.

- The barriers a compensation culture puts up between citizens is very unwelcome. Adults become shy of children. Volunteers veer away from work where they expose themselves to lawsuits. Ordinary, unqualified helpers are disempowered because they have to wait for experts or qualified professionals. Experience and common sense are no longer considered suitable grounds for action. A legally sensitive passer-by will watch someone die rather than help them out of trouble.

- If this is all 'got up by the media' it shouldn't be too hard to put out accurate counterpropaganda. The whole area is so fraught with politics, vested interests and hidden agendas that no figures or statements can be taken at face value.

- Let's have a cadre of special policemen who sign up for the difficult and psychologically dangerous work. They will be men and women who go into buildings before a risk assessment is complete. They will risk their lives and their mental health for the good of the public. They will be given privileges, training and special assistance – but they will prize valour before prudence. Their *esprit de corps* will be more like the armed forces than their civilian equivalents.

- Rough contact sports should be brought back into the curriculum on a daily basis, especially for boys who want to play such games. They burn off aggression. And fat. Properly taught, they develop ideas of fairness and courage under fire. Superficial injuries to children should be made light of.

- The introduction of lawyers to the normal social and professional interchange is never the best idea. Most claims can be assessed very much more quickly and easily than the current system allows. Why does everything take so long and cost so much? Because that's how the incentives are lined up. Lawyers are paid by the hour. That's why miners' lawyers got thousands of pounds and offered (in one case in 2006) £7.30 to a miner who suffered from lung disease. An ordinary 'slip-and-trip' claim should take a morning to prepare (including the site visit to photograph the obstruction).

- Why should sensitive or cowardly people get bigger pay-outs than sturdy, resilient or braver people? They've been hurt more, but does that mean they should be compensated more? Why should courage attract a penalty?

These questions go on and on. It's an intricate, complex question. But culture is intricate and complex. No doubt there's a good deal of to and fro to go through yet. I hope this book has helped feed something into that argument.